Disasters and Social Reproduction

Mapping Social Reproduction Theory

Series editors Tithi Bhattacharya, Professor of South Asian History and the Director of Global Studies at Purdue University; and Susan Ferguson, Associate Professor, Faculty of Liberal Arts, Wilfrid Laurier University

Capitalism is a system of exploitation and oppression. This series uses the insights of Social Reproduction Theory to deepen our understanding of the intimacy of that relationship, and the contradictions within it, past and present. The books include empirical investigations of the ways in which social oppressions of race, sexuality, ability, gender and more inhabit, shape and are shaped by the processes of creating labour power for capital. The books engage a critical exploration of Social Reproduction, enjoining debates about the theoretical and political tools required to challenge capitalism today.

Also available

Social Reproduction Theory:
Remapping Class, Recentering Oppression
Edited by Tithi Bhattacharya

A Feminist Reading of Debt
Luci Cavallero and Verónica Gago

Women and Work:
Feminism, Labour, and Social Reproduction
Susan Ferguson

Social Reproduction Theory and the Socialist Horizon:
Work, Power and Political Strategy
Aaron Jaffe

Disasters and Social Reproduction

Crisis Response Between the State and Community

Peer Illner

PLUTO PRESS

First published 2021 by Pluto Press
345 Archway Road, London N6 5AA

www.plutobooks.com

Copyright © Peer Illner 2021

The right of Peer Illner to be identified as the author of this work has been asserted in accordance with the Copyright, Designs and Patents Act 1988.

British Library Cataloguing in Publication Data
A catalogue record for this book is available from the British Library

ISBN   978 0 7453 3955 9   Hardback
ISBN   978 0 7453 3954 2   Paperback
ISBN   978 1 7868 0550 8   PDF eBook
ISBN   978 1 7868 0552 2   Kindle eBook
ISBN   978 1 7868 0551 5   EPUB eBook

This book is printed on paper suitable for recycling and made from fully managed and sustained forest sources. Logging, pulping and manufacturing processes are expected to conform to the environmental standards of the country of origin.

Typeset by Stanford DTP Services, Northampton, England

Simultaneously printed in the United Kingdom and United States of America

For Lianna

Contents

Acknowledgements

This book would have not seen the light of day without the many labours – paid and unpaid – of a number of people and institutions. It is to them I wish to express my gratitude. I would like to thank the Department of Arts and Cultural Studies at the University of Copenhagen for having hosted me during the early stages of my research. Thank you to Mikkel Bolt Rasmussen and Isak Winkel Holm, under whose generous supervision the seeds for this project were sown. Also at Copenhagen, I am grateful to the members of the 'Changing Disasters' research group for the stimulating conversations, comradely disagreements, and for offering me a forum to develop my ideas. Generous institutional backing in the later stages of writing was provided by the Research Centre 'Normative Orders' at Goethe University, Frankfurt. I wish to thank my colleagues there for having supported my research throughout.

I have benefitted tremendously from the comments and feedback of Jasper Bernes, Joshua Clover, Mark Neocleous, Devika Sharma, Maya Gonzales, and the participants of the Historical Materialism Conferences at the American University, Beirut in 2017 and at SOAS, University of London in 2018. Heartfelt thanks must also go to my students at the University of Copenhagen, Goethe University, Frankfurt and the Architectural Association, London. Their curiosity, fresh eyes and continued interest enabled me to stay curious myself. I am grateful to the external readers of the manuscript, whose questions, criticisms and queries greatly improved it; in particular Susan Ferguson, Tithi Bhattacharya and an anonymous reviewer. At Pluto Press, I would like to thank David Shulman for his sure-handed guidance of the project from proposal to publication, for his tireless work and enduring enthusiasm; Robert Webb for seeing the book through production and Carrie Giunta for her insightful edits.

For their friendship during the time of writing, my thanks to Bruno Seffen, Octave Perrault, Evan Saarinen, Lucas Liccini, Felix Lennert, Sebastian Glowacki and Alison Hugill. Finally, thank you is not enough to express how grateful I am to Lianna Mark for her love and support and for being there – in disaster and crisis, but above all, beyond.

Parts of Chapter 5 first appeared as 'Who's Calling the Emergency? The Black Panthers, Securitisation and the Question of Identity' in *Culture Unbound* 7(3), 479–95. An earlier version of Chapter 7 was published as 'The Locals do it Better? The Strange Victory of Occupy Sandy' in *Eco-Culture: Disaster, Narrative, Discourse*, R. Bell and R. Ficociello, Lanham, Lexington Books, 49–72.

1

2005: The Unclaimed Corpses

Racism [. . .] is the state-sanctioned or extralegal production and exploitation of group-differentiated vulnerability to premature death.
— Ruth Wilson Gilmore

THE CORPSE IN THE STREET

On 11 September 2005, two weeks after Hurricane Katrina inundated New Orleans, killing at least 1,836 people[1] and destroying much of the city infrastructure, the news network *Democracy Now* uncovered a scandal that aggravated New Orleanians well beyond the immediate impact of the hurricane: the scandal of dead bodies, rotting in the street. The live broadcast showed an unclaimed corpse, and, standing next to it, Malik Rahim, resident of the neighbourhood of Algiers and founder of the Common Ground network, engaged in the reconstruction of New Orleans. For days, Rahim had been asking city authorities, from the police to the army to the National Guard, to remove an unidentified dead body from the roadside. 'The kids pass by and they're seeing it,' says Rahim:

His body been here for almost two weeks. Two weeks tomorrow [. . .] that this man's body been lying here. And there's no reason for it. Look where we at? I mean, it's not flooded. There's no reason for them to be—left that body right here like this [. . .] Every day, we ask them about coming and pick it up. And they refuse to come and pick it up. And you could see, it's literally decomposing right here. Right out in the sun. Every day we sit up and we ask them about it. Because, I mean, this is close as you could get to tropical climate in America. And they won't do anything with it. (cited in Goodman, 2015: min. 49:02)

With Algiers being one of the most heavily policed areas of New Orleans, each city authority in turn drives by the dead body, as if on command.

When confronted by the show's anchor Amy Goodman and her camera, they admit to knowing about the body but deny any responsibility in removing it from the site. The Algiers corpse was no isolated case. It later emerged that the retrieval of dead bodies started in earnest only on 9 September, a good ten days after Katrina struck New Orleans. With elderly people of colour in the African American neighbourhoods of the Lower Ninth Ward and Lakeview constituting the vast majority of disaster victims, black residents were left to reckon with the wreckage, with the smell of their decomposing neighbours infesting the tropical air.

Those same rotting bodies ignored by city authorities make manifest the systematic omission in scholarly attempts to make sense of events. While critical accounts have focused on how pre-existing social injustices made African American New Orleanians disproportionately vulnerable to hurricane damage (Laska and Morrow, 2006; Tierney, 2006; Brunsma, 2010), on how the federal rescue operations were influenced by racial prejudice (Tierney, Bevc et al., 2006; Russill and Lavin, 2011) or on how the Bush administration used the disaster to advance neoliberal pro-business reforms (Klein, 2007; Adams, 2012; Adams, 2013), a thorough analysis of disaster relief as a question of who clears out the dead remained conspicuously absent. Filling the analytic gap that was left behind when the waters retreated, this book is dedicated to answering that question. It argues that disasters are primarily a problem for social reproduction, understood, following political theorist Nancy Fraser, as 'the capacities available for birthing and raising children, caring for friends and family members, maintaining households and broader communities' (2017:21).

In this view, disaster relief becomes a form of reproductive labour, akin to childcare, elder care or gravedigging, and indeed often involving all three. When seen through the lens of social reproduction, disasters pose the question of who should perform these elemental tasks. This question touches on the fundamental distinction between the state and civil society,[2] thus challenging political life as we know it. This book argues that, far from being an exception, the handling of disaster victims by neighbours and relatives during Hurricane Katrina exemplifies a wider trend. In America today, disaster relief is increasingly shouldered by civil society, in an attempt to make up for the state's reluctance to deliver this essential service.

A thorough theorisation of relief work as a form of reproductive labour is as yet still missing. Little has been written on the structural transformations of the disaster aid sector, including the changing roles of the state and civil society in the face of disaster. Instead, from the 1755 Lisbon earthquake to Hurricane Katrina, from 9/11 to the 2010 Haitian earthquake, the element of each disaster that researchers most often pick out and focus on is the disruptive, natural event. Between the metaphysical investigations of the Lisbon rubble and today's elaborate contingency planning, a disaster is commonly framed as an exceptional 'moment of interruption and novelty' (Aradau and van Munster, 2011:10) that ruptures an otherwise 'normal' state of affairs.

The New Orleans corpses alert us, however, to a different dimension of disaster. They highlight disasters' *longue durée*, epitomised by the dead body that simply remains, rotting and ignored by the state. They alert us to the structural issues of poverty and racism that create the conditions in which certain communities will not only be lastingly affected by disaster, but also made responsible for managing their own misfortune. The African American disaster victims rotting in the sun represent instances of 'death by class' and 'death by race', rather than the officially certified 'death by flood'. The difference between these views is neatly summed up in the pilot episode of David Simon's HBO series *Tremé*: 'What hit the Mississippi Gulf Coast was a natural disaster, a hurricane pure and simple. The flooding of New Orleans was a man-made catastrophe, a federal fuck-up of epic proportions' (cited in Holm, 2012:15).

This book seeks to illuminate the underlying dynamics of this and other federal 'fuck-ups'. Instead of seeing disaster as a 'natural' contingency, it proposes a fully socialised definition of disaster as a crisis-point, arising from the interaction between capitalism's ecologic degradation and the organised neglect of the state. In this view, rather than being the hapless victims of natural calamity, communities suffer the combined effects of capitalism's unsustainable exploitation of nature and the interventionist depravation wrought by the state. In keeping with the ethos of social reproduction theory that 'displays an analytical irreverence to "visible facts" and privileges "process" instead' (Bhattacharya, 2017:2), I argue for an understanding of disaster not as a single moment, but as an unfolding, in which natural crises, do not create, but rather expose ongoing social crises. Nature is thus understood, not as a chaotic antagonist to the social world, but as the product of a complex nature-human relationship. In short, I contend that the origins of 'natural' disasters are never purely natural.

Whilst the critique of an overly literal understanding of the 'natural' causes of disaster has gained traction, in the age of anthropogenic climate change, within disaster studies and beyond (Quarantelli, 1978; Hewitt, 1983; Blaikie, Cannon et al., 1994), this scholarship remains plagued by a significant shortcoming. Question as it may the natural origins of disasters, it often relies, in turn, on a simplistic notion of the social, in which a disaster's impact on a community is seen as a straightforward interface between a calamity and the social fabric, which is itself taken for granted (Solnit, 2009; Patterson, Weil and Patel, 2010; Twigg and Mosel, 2017). By relying on an ahistorical understanding of the social, this critique ignores how state policy, or lack thereof, has historically contoured the social realm. The effort to denaturalise nature, in other words, gives rise to a naturalising of society. By combining natural and social analysis in a thoroughgoing examination of the labour process, social reproduction theory offers us a way out of this dilemma, surpassing simplistic assumptions about the role of nature and society in disasters.

Social reproduction theory builds on Marxist analyses of the irreconcilability of capitalism's ecologic and economic processes. Rather than positing humanity as distinctly separate from nature, Karl Marx argued for a 'metabolic relation' between the social and the natural, in which all human activity springs from nature and must ultimately return to it. The key to humanity's interaction with nature is Marx's notion of labour, understood as the process by which humans use nature's resources to reproduce themselves. For Marx, labour is a transhistorical faculty, encompassing all 'practical human activity' (1984:111). In volume one of *Capital*, he writes:

Labour is, first of all, a process between man and nature, a process by which man, through his own actions, mediates, regulates and controls the metabolism between himself and nature [. . .] He sets in motion the natural forces which belong to his own body, his arms, legs, head and hands, in order to appropriate the materials of nature in a form adapted to his own needs. Through this movement he acts upon external nature and changes it, and in this way he simultaneously changes his own nature [. . .] It [the labor process] is the universal condition for the metabolic interaction between man and nature, the everlasting nature-imposed condition of human existence. (1976:283, 290)

While labour itself may be the transhistorical mediation of humanity's relationship to nature, the specific conditions under which humans work the land and adapt it to their particular needs varies a great deal. The peculiarity of capitalist labour is that it uses nature's resources in an unsustainable way, producing what the sociologist John Bellamy Foster (1999) has called a 'metabolic rift' in the exchange between humans and nature.[3]

If in Marx's understanding of the labour process nature appears as dynamic and malleable, so then does society. As humans belabour nature, their interactions with the natural world also create the systems, institutions and structures that make up their social world. For social reproduction theorist Susan Ferguson, 'human labour or work – the practical, conscious interaction between people and the natural world of which they are part – creates the social processes and relations that, in turn, determine the processes and relations of that labour' (2020:16). In other words, from the perspective of social reproduction, there is nothing abstract about society. It does not exist on account of its institutions, its electoral system or its citizen rights. Instead, for this bottom-up approach, the social is constantly made and remade through reproductive acts of labour.

Marx's labour lens is important because it surpasses the facile binary between natural and social causes of calamity, allowing us to see disasters as the outcome of a risk-prone mode of production and reproduction. It widens our understanding of disaster by drawing attention to the systemic way in which our capitalist mode of production – at the same time as it produces our social and economic world – also produces our disasters. While today it has become more popular to think of capitalism as damaging to the environment, this is mostly done in the guise of a circumstantial critique of certain areas of capitalist production – such as fossil fuels or nuclear energy – rather than as a structural critique of the capitalist economy in its entirety.[4] Faithful to Marx's insight that 'men must be in position to live in order to be able to "make history"' (1970:48), this book argues that in the late twentieth century, our 'position to live' was cast into severe crisis, following the reshuffling of social reproductive tasks from the state sector to the market and the community.[5] The following is an attempt to make sense of this crisis through the changes it wrought onto disaster relief.

To date, most critical disaster research has focused on what has come to be known as 'disaster capitalism' (Klein, 2007; Loewenstein, 2017), i.e. the ways in which the neoliberal state has privatised relief services to advance the business interests of commercial operators. This book is dedicated to the opposite question: How has the withdrawal of the state from emergency relief forced communities to perform disaster aid on a voluntary basis and free of charge? While the commercialisation of social reproductive services under austerity is well understood, the concomitant extension of the voluntary sector to perform those tasks, which both the state and the private sector have abandoned, has not been sufficiently studied. As we will see, many social-reproductive services during disasters resist commercialisation because they do not yield sufficient profits. These services skip the market and pass directly from state to the community.

Yet when looking at the recent budgetary figures of the United States' Federal Emergency Management Agency FEMA, the withdrawal of the state from disaster relief is glaringly obvious. During the 2012 US presidential election, voters could choose between a 3% cut to the FEMA budget, proposed by the Obama camp and a 40% cut, suggested by the Romney camp (Khimm, 2012: para. 4–8). More recently, President Trump redirected $10 million from FEMA to the US immigration enforcement agency's detention program (Stanley-Becker, 2018: para.1). The trend is clear: as each year records a new spike in disasters (Guha-Sapir, Hoyois et al., 2015:4), budgetary cuts are implemented across the political spectrum. As with other reductions to public spending, the hole left behind by the axing of state budgets has been filled by private investors, seeking to capitalise on insurances and disaster aid, as well as by unpaid members from civil society, who perform formerly state-run services out of goodwill and free of charge.

Coextensive with this federal withdrawal, scientific studies of disaster began to flaunt the emergent and self-organising potential of civil society to become resilient to disasters and survive alone and without the state during emergencies (Hilhorst, 2004; Wisner, Gaillard et al., 2012; Kelman, Burns et al., 2015). This book challenges the current state of disaster research by arguing that most disaster studies have ignored the economic dimension of the 'resilience turn'. The consequence of this omission is that the interdisciplinary field fails to grasp the systematic reconfiguration of social life that has taken place in the last decades of the twentieth century.

I contend that developing an account that is sensitive to the disastrous effects that the state's withdrawal from emergency relief has had on communities requires coupling the notion of disaster with that of social reproduction. This coupling allows us to de-escalate disasters; to see them not as shock events but as an everyday problem of reproductive labour. Concretely, I argue that the reshuffling of disaster relief from the sphere of the federal state to that of civil society unfolded as a crucial response to the economic crisis of the 1970s. It was then, after a period of incremental state involvement, beginning with the 1803 Portsmouth fire (Farber and Chen, 2006:102),[6] that the federal government withdrew from the provision of disaster aid, in an attempt to lower the state deficit.

THE SHORT AMERICAN CENTURY

Focusing on what I call the 'short American century' between 1920 and 2020, this book develops a historical and theoretical account that maps the relationship between the federal state and disaster relief onto the unfolding economic crisis. In four extensive case studies and a shorter postscript, I trace disaster aid's pendulum swing from becoming a federal responsibility in the 1930s in response to the Great Depression to becoming increasingly cast off in the 1970s in response to mid-century stagflation.[7] After examining the gradual integration of disaster aid into the remit of state-led social reproduction during the New Deal, I argue that the US government reacted to the decline in its productive power by resolutely scaling back social spending in all areas from housing to disaster relief, creating a situation of austerity,[8] in which diverse forms of reproductive labour increasingly have to be carried out by the people themselves. After decades of steadily growing investment into federal disaster aid, and despite a strong increase in natural and man-made disasters, the state sector is today increasingly withdrawing from the provision of relief services.

Since the 1970s, we are thus confronted with the following double-movement, relative to the spheres of the state and civil society. On the state level, a movement of integration, in which formerly specialist authority on disasters is relinquished and the vernacular skills and capacities of the people are drawn on during calamities. On the social level, a moment of exclusion, indexed by cuts to social spending and the exponentially rising unemployment that raised the number of so-called surplus populations, those permanently excluded from wage labour, to staggering dimensions. The inclusion on the level of participatory policies is thus undergirded by a growing and profound exclusion of people from the basic possibility of reproducing themselves. Let me reformulate this development as a hypothesis regarding emergencies today: Since the economic crisis of the 1970s, disasters have served as occasions that absorb the reproductive labour of surplus populations as unwaged inputs, allowing the US state to cut back on social spending. While this development is a disaster for civil society, since it exposes communities to fend for themselves without support by the state, it is also, potentially, a disaster for the state, since austerity at the same time creates the forces that may contest it.

The following case studies seek to elucidate this dialectic. They show how political struggles around disasters are fundamentally struggles around the spheres and responsibilities of the public and the private, the waged and the unwaged, the state and the people. They thus impact the very structural foundations of social life, as we know it. Concretely, they make visible the double movement of the inclusion of citizens into disaster relief and the coextensive exclusion of populations from the possibility of reproducing themselves, while documenting their struggles to maintain their lives and livelihoods. Therefore, as much as this is a book about disasters, it is also a book about how the left grappled with the politics of social reproduction throughout the twentieth century. Through the lens of disaster aid, it charts the trajectory of social reproduction from its marginalisation by the official labour politics of the 1930s, to its centrality in the revolutionary movements of the 1970s and in the new millennium's quest for revolutionary commons.[9]

Taking disaster relief as its focal point, the book joins in the unfinished 'process of rewriting a general narrative of capitalism, class composition and state formation in the United States from the perspective of social reproduction' (Mohandesi and Teitelman, 2017:38). Posing the question of socialist politics throughout, I argue that in the twentieth century, social reproduction became a dominant arena in which socialists struggled with capital and the state over the value of life. Contrary to industrial antagonisms, the state emerged as a major player on this new battleground by first extending state-led social reproduction initiatives under the New Deal and then retracting them under 1970s stagflation and 2000s austerity. The ensuing crisis in reproduction forced the left to constantly adapt its tactics; an endeavour in which it sometimes succeeded and sometimes failed. The following chapters illustrate the reproductive antagonism between capital, labour and the state through the prism of disaster relief.

The book begins in the 1920s with the integration of disaster relief into state-led social reproduction during President Roosevelt's New Deal and in the immediate post-war era. I argue that federalising disaster aid served the purpose of creating employment in an ailing economic environment, as well as generating opportunities for infrastructural development. By examining the federal state's handling of the early twentieth century hurricane season in Florida, I show how the presence of a strong Keynesian state initially formed the relation between the state and civil society into a temporary union of shared interests.

Following the historical arc into the 1960s, the second comprehensive case study examines the mid-century watershed in the administration of American social reproduction. While, following desegregation, the federal state extended its welfare profile to formerly marginalised communities under Lyndon B. Johnson's Great Society programmes, militant social movements began providing their own model of community-led social reproduction in response to the state's failure to live up to its promises of employment and prosperity. This chapter examines how the self-organised social reproduction initiatives of the Black Panther Party for Self-Defense fostered community life in conditions of endemic violence. While this violence was structural and not event-bound, defying spectacular notions of disaster, its responses similarly defy vulnerability studies' schema of adaptation and resilience. The chapter examines the spread of a politics of social reproduction on both sides of the state/civil society divide, analysing how the terrain of social reproduction gradually replaced industrial labour struggles as a primary arena of political antagonism.

The third case study moves into the 1990s and travels East to examine the 1995 Chicago Heat Wave. Reviewing disaster scholars' singling out of Chicago's high crime rate as a primary vulnerability factor, I firstly show how it was not high rates of crime, but the Clinton era austerity politics that contributed to the disproportionately high death rate of senior citizens during the heat wave. Arguing that the rollback of state-led social reproduction in the 1990s created a reproductive vacuum that was not filled by community-run initiatives, I secondly demonstrate that the 1990s rise in crime is a symptom of this gap in social reproduction, making high levels of senior mortality and youth crime the two defining poles of the 1990s reproductive crisis.

The fourth case study addresses the role of community-based disaster relief during the 2012 Superstorm Sandy. Since the vulnerability turn of the 1970s, disaster studies has vocally advanced citizen participation as a powerful tool for building community resilience (Bankoff, Frerks et al., 2004; Cutter, Ahern et al., 2013; Tierney, 2014; Patel, Rogers et al., 2017). Much is made of the field's turn away from technocratic state authority and its affirmation of local, embedded and decentralised aid practices in the fight against disasters. The case study complicates this progressive narrative. It examines the exemplary case of Occupy Sandy, a large-scale, self-organised relief initiative, launched by the social movement Occupy Wall Street in response to Superstorm Sandy. It firstly discusses Occupy Sandy's presence as the most successful relief provider on the ground, far surpassing the efficacy of the Red Cross and of FEMA. Secondly, it reflects on the counter-intuitive endorsement of the group by the government agency, the Department of Homeland Security. Situating the bizarre proximity between anarchist social movement and governmental mega-institution in the context of the continued withdrawal of the US state from the provision of social reproductive services, the chapter finally reflects on the political currency of vulnerability and its role within a new configuration between the state and civil society in times of austerity.

In a concluding postscript, I turn to the current Coronavirus crisis to examine the relationship between the federal state and the many mutual aid initiatives that emerged in response to the pandemic. Marshalling a social reproduction approach, I firstly argue that, confronted with the state's systemic failure to prepare for and mitigate the consequences of the virus outbreak, mutual aid was called upon to fill the gaps in the state's service provision. Secondly, by situating disaster vulnerability within the intergenerational transmission of health risks, I show how a social reproduction framework reveals the deep-seated socio-economic factors that led African Americans to experience elevated vulnerability to Covid-19. Thirdly, I examine how the recent wave of political protests in the US addressed the layered crises of both Coronavirus vulnerability and police violence, marking out social reproduction as the arena of current and future class and race conflict.

Before beginning the task of mapping the changes to the relief sector, let us ask why disasters are so often understood as exceptional moments, rather than as structural conditions. Asking this allows us to measure the urgency of a social reproduction approach to disasters.

2

Vulnerability Beyond Resilience

Katrina offered us a vision of the future, and it is not a resilient one.

— Kathleen Tierney

BOMBS AND OTHER DISASTERS

Why are disasters so often understood as sudden, rupturing events? In order to depart from the impasse of an event-based conception of emergency, I argue that disaster studies' history has to be reconstructed materialistically. Establishing itself in the post-war climate of the 1950s and taking shape during the Cold War, the scientific study of disasters began in a wartime context that sought to understand and control crowd behaviour during enemy bombardments. The very first recorded 'disaster investigation' was the United States Strategic Bombing Survey, which studied the impact of the allied bombardment of Japanese and European cities (Iklé, 1951; Spangrud, 1987; Davis, 2002). Systematising this research and extending it from military applications to the civilian domain, the National Opinion Research Center at the University of Chicago conducted a series of studies on infrastructure accidents such as airplane crashes, but also on various fires and an earthquake. In 1952, the Disaster Research Group was founded at the National Research Council, to survey the current state of disaster research (Williams, 1954; Perry, 2007), making it the first ever disaster research centre. In this way, the experience of war became the template for our perception of the most diverse kinds of natural and man-made disasters.

The scientific paradigm through which disasters were then understood was cybernetics, an interdisciplinary research field that studies socio-technological systems and their interactions with other systems, their so-called feedback. The philosopher of science, Peter Galison, describes how Norbert Wiener, physics extraordinaire and military advisor, 'coined the term cybernetics in the summer of 1947 to designate what he hoped would be a new science of control mechanisms in which the exchange of information would play a central role' (1994:232). Concretely, what was supposed to be controlled was anti-aircraft fire and crowd behaviour in urban environments, beleaguered by German bombers. While early cyberneticists looked at systems as closed and centralised, the experience of Nazi bombardments in Britain, and fear of its growing possibility in the US, caused a strong interest in decentralised systems, creating the sprawling suburb with no localisable centre as a defence strategy in its wake (Galison, 2001).[10] As the history of the cybernetic paradigm evolved in an attempt to control evermore amorphous and diffuse networks, the way in which disasters were understood as disruptions to complex systems evolved with it. However, while disaster scholars themselves make much out of distancing themselves from their control room origins, their emphasis on predicting contingencies and regulating population response is very much in keeping with cybernetics' militarised focus on crowd control.

The bombs on Dresden, Hiroshima and Nagasaki thus became a laboratory for American emergency planning or, in the language of the emerging disaster scholars, they became templates for 'a failure of a social system to deliver reasonable conditions of life' (Perry, 2007:5). Based on research into crowd behaviour by social psychologists and sociologists, influenced by systems theory, disaster studies established itself as a discipline in close connection with the government and the military with the goal of researching past contingencies in order to contain future threats. At the time of a nationally cultivated fear of a Soviet nuclear attack, the new disasters centres' task was to better predict the likelihood and the effects of contingencies and develop policies to build resilience. Research into disasters was therefore always tied to behavioural protocols, suggesting a normative reordering of population response, according to 'exceptions' and 'exception routines', in which 'disasters are fundamentally disruptions of routines' (Stallings, 1998:136).

Summing up the last 70 years of disaster research, a recent review article defines the field as follows:

Disaster studies address the social and behavioural aspects of sudden onset collective stress situations typically referred to as mass emergencies or disaster. These situations can be created by natural hazards, technological accidents, violent intergroup conflicts, shortages of vital resources and other major hazards to life, health, property, well-being and everyday routines. (Lindell, 2013:798)

Despite the variety of situations Lindell counts as disasters, all of his scenarios are envisioned as 'sudden' disturbances to an established system. This 'figure of time' (Juengel, 2009:443), in which an unexpected exception ruptures a 'normal' rule, configures the imaginary of everyday ordinariness confronted with an eruptive event that has become characteristic of our view of disaster. It assumes that society follows an established and calm course that is occasionally and spectacularly interrupted by a sudden occurrence.

CHALLENGING THE EVENT:
FROM CENTRALISED TO DECENTRALISED CONTROL

In the 1970s, this technocratic view of disaster as a disruptive event, necessitating a mainly technical solution was challenged. US geographers, loosely affiliated with second-order cybernetics,[11] developed a so-called hazards approach (Burton and Kates, 1964; Burton, Kates et al., 1993) that, rather than only looking at a disaster's effects on the ground, sought to understand the environmental and man-made triggers that caused disasters. This school defined disaster as 'the interface between an extreme physical event and a vulnerable human population' (Susman, O'Keefe et al., 1983:264). Following on in this vein, the geographer Kenneth Hewitt argued in 1983 that it was insufficient to view disasters merely as geophysical occurrences that disrupted an otherwise normal state of affairs (Hewitt, 1983; Hewitt, 1997). Disasters were rather, he proposed, the result of social action and social processes. They were thus thoroughly anthropogenic in nature and their timescale extended far beyond the immediacy of a singular event.

With this, Hewitt ushered in the so-called vulnerability approach that dominates sociological and anthropological disaster research today. The vulnerability framework extends the analytic gaze beyond the immediacy of the disaster onto the social, cultural, political, and ecological conditions that played a role in its production or exacerbated its severity (Blaikie, Cannon et al., 1994; Bankoff, Frerks et al., 2004; Wisner, Gaillard et al., 2012; Tierney, 2014). Formerly seen in technocratic terms as a contingent event that necessitated a swift, mainly technical solution, disasters were until the 1980s talked about in a vocabulary that effaced their social logic. The vulnerability approach argued, on the contrary, that disasters are the result of underlying conditions of social vulnerability coupled with an external hazard. In the paradigmatic definition of Blaikie, Cannon, Davis and Wisner: 'By vulnerability we mean the characteristics of a person or group and their situation that influence their capacity to anticipate, cope with, resist and recover from the impact of a natural hazard (an extreme natural event or process)' (2004:11).

For vulnerability scholars, this holds true for whichever kind of disaster we are talking about. Rather than resulting from forces of nature or failures in technology, disasters are in this perspective always the effect of a particular configuration of the social that cumulatively produces a disaster over time. Hewitt's path breaking work of the 1980s was continued by Dennis Mileti, who developed a holistic perspective on disasters that starts from vulnerability and highlights the production of disasters in interconnected social and natural environments. By highlighting the social components that produce disasters, the vulnerability approach emphasised the political responsibility of power holders and decision-makers. Sharpening this social responsibility, Mileti argued that all disasters are the result of decisions that organisations 'make or fail to make' (1999:39).

Starting from the assumption of social root causes for disaster, the vulnerability approach greatly extended the analytic horizon of disaster research by privileging an analysis of social structure over the rupturing event. This structural view has also enabled a politicisation of the field. Taking a critical stance towards the capitalist tenets of development, free trade and competition, the vulnerability approach argues that if today 75% of disasters worldwide occur in the global South (Bankoff and Hilhorst, 2004:3), this is due to capitalist hegemony and development aggression, forcing local communities to adapt to fierce competition, thereby causing widespread damage to the environment. For sociologist Eric Klinenberg (1999), the zooming-out movement of the vulnerability approach makes it possible to 'denaturalise' disasters and tease out their underlying political economy. In this context, disaster scholars Greg Bankoff and Dorothea Hilhorst have pointed out that the exposure of vulnerable communities to disaster most often follows established power relations of class, race and gender. The unequal exposure to disaster is thus 'largely a function of the power relations operative in every society' (Bankoff and Hilhorst, 2004:2).

SELF-HELP HELL

While vulnerability scholars regard the move from seeing disaster as an external contingency to considering social causes for disaster as progressive, I argue that disaster studies' household theory of vulnerability is not sensitive to the way in which disaster vulnerability emerges as a systemic corollary of capitalist everyday life. This becomes obvious when looking at the way in which disaster studies remains tied to classical notions of event-bound harm that ultimately curtail its analytic depth. If vulnerability scholars have conducted in-depth analyses of unequal social, political, ecological and economic conditions, they have paradoxically limited the impact of their rich, structural studies by always relating them back to the exposure to a momentary disaster, now called hazard. They have thus held on to the normative idea of a more or less stable everyday state that is impacted by a sudden disruption. For vulnerability studies, the disruption may have been decades in the making, however, its onset is still imagined as sudden and unexpected.

This creates a paradoxical situation, in which vulnerability studies' detailed investigations into structural inequality are *only* relevant insofar as these conditions expose communities to a possible external hazard. While the innovation of vulnerability studies lay precisely in drawing attention to the *structural* dimension of disasters, they too quickly return to a hazards-perspective that casts their entire research in light of a spectacular event or tipping point,[12] at which previously tolerable conditions are framed as intolerable.

By offering a circumstantial critique of the way in which power holders expose some communities to disaster, while keeping others safe, vulnerability studies misses the systemic nature, in which power structures make populations vulnerable; not only in disaster, but in everyday life. Paraphrasing the geographer Ruth Wilson Gilmore, we can say that disasters highlight 'the production [. . .] of group-differentiated vulnerability to premature death' (2002:261) that characterises populations' day to day life, rather than representing its exception. If vulnerability studies restricts itself to naming isolated risk factors, a social reproduction approach to disaster connects these particulars by showing their shared conditions of emergence in a common mode of production and reproduction. Furthermore, rather than merely tying supposedly random events together, this historical-materialist approach identifies their underlying connection and emphasises the need for systemic change to address and prevent disasters.

Vulnerability studies shies away from any such mention of systemic change. We can see this when looking at the discipline's proposed solution attempts to diminish disaster vulnerability. Arguing that the seeds of community vulnerability lie not only in the global (mis)distribution of wealth, but also in embedded structures of community life, the framework promotes a self-help approach that places the responsibility to improve vulnerable conditions squarely within the community itself. Researchers on Hurricane Katrina, for instance, have argued that the excessive vulnerability of black residents during the flooding of New Orleans was due to the high numbers of African American renters who had to rely on the goodwill of landlords to provide safe and flood-proof housing (Laska and Morrow, 2006).

This perspective promotes private, owner-occupied housing as a path to safety, since it is assumed that homeowners act more responsibly in maintaining a safe domestic environment. Contesting this endorsement of homeownership, Fussell, Sastry and VanLandingham (2010) have shown that it was black *homeowners* in particular who bore the brunt of the destruction and experienced far greater housing damage than white residents, often making them unable to return to New Orleans post-Katrina. Indeed, the push towards privatisation in the 1980s and 1990s often encouraged tenants in urban areas to buy property on low-lying, unsafe ground. Furthermore, the necessity to insure a private home, made house owners purchase hurricane insurance but often no flood insurance, since their municipality had reassured them that New Orleans would not be flooded again.

Here, vulnerability scholars, who advocate homeownership as a strategy to build disaster resilience are proven wrong, since it was precisely *privatisation* that caused disproportionate housing damage to African American residents. In his in-depth study on the privatisation of public housing in New Orleans, the sociologist John Arena hammers another nail into the coffin of vulnerability studies' credo of responsibility through entrepreneurship. Arena shows how the sell-off of public housing was essentially carried out not by local governments, but by non-profit tenant organisations in cooperation with large real estate firms. He describes how the discourse of privatisation was shared by real estate firms and social movements alike, who promoted a view in which disaster victims were themselves seen as responsible for their damage:

Tenant management would provide public housing residents, Mayor Moria explained, with 'the social and psychological benefits of self-determination and the acceptance of responsibility' [. . .] and would therefore help wean them off government dependence. This line of thinking was wholly consistent with the racialized self-help ideology that increasingly took hold in the 1980s in the context of Reaganite retrenchment. The message to African Americans was clear: the solutions and sources of the social problems they faced – such as lack of jobs and housing – were rooted in their communities. (2012:57–8)

PRODUCING DISASTERS, PROMOTING RESILIENCE?[13]

Arena's study is provocative in that it challenges the most dearly held assumption within vulnerability studies, namely that individuals and groups should self-organise and assume responsibility to become resilient to disasters. Resilience is a concept originating in ecology that is today applied in a variety of contexts from psychology to organisational theory to sports and military theory. Resilience designates the capacity of a system to withstand strain and pressure without incurring fatal damage. Being a descriptive as well as a normative term, resilient structures are flexible in that they can persevere in a variety of environments without needing excessive resources for their survival. Resilience privileges subjects and communities who manage to make do with very little, in times when resources are scarce. The 100 Resilient Cities initiative funded by the Rockefeller Foundation and launched in 2013 lists different factors that make cities 'survive and thrive' regardless of the challenge (2013: para. 5). The Foundation suggests that resilient cities are flexible, i.e. they easily adapt to constantly changing environments, in which disruption is the norm. They are resourceful, meaning they possess optimal resource allocation under conditions of scarcity. Finally, they are robust in that they possess durable systems that can withstand prolonged stress. Political theorist Mark Neocleous explains the basic mechanism of resilience: 'Stemming from the idea of a system and originating in ecological thought, the term connotes the capacity of a system to return to a previous state, to recover from a shock, or to bounce back after a crisis or trauma' (2013:3).

In disaster studies, vulnerability and resilience imply each other. If communities are diagnosed as vulnerable to disasters due to structural conditions of income inequality, racial discrimination and economic marginalisation, for disaster studies, the way out of these conditions is not resistance, i.e. political organising that targets the root causes of this predicament in an attempt to change it, but adaptation and resilience. Becoming resilient is a coping strategy. It accepts that marginalised populations are disproportionately exposed to suffering and harm and entices victims to become active in overcoming their damage. Rather than collectively trying to change the situation in which the damage was incurred, it rewards communities who manage to overcome their predicament individually, while leaving its causes untouched. For political theorist Julian Reid, a resilient subject is 'a subject that accepts the disastrousness of the world it lives in as a condition for partaking in that world' (2013:355). Resilient subjects have 'accepted the imperative not to resist or secure themselves from the dangers they face but instead adapt to their enabling conditions' (ibid.).

Moreover, this personal overcoming becomes a yardstick that measures success. Communities that successfully become resilient to their harmful milieu are rewarded with status and capital gains. Those communities or individuals who do not manage to overcome their damage are left behind and shamed for not being *resilient enough*. If resilience were a movie genre, it would be film noir, presenting a dark and gritty world that rewards those, sharp-witted enough to develop survival tactics to get by. If it were a rap album it would be 50 Cent's *Get Rich or Die Trying*, which turns economic deprivation into a resource for aspirational success. As an attitude, its character is captured by what architect and political theorist Eyal Weizman calls 'the politics of lesser evil' (2011), a hard-nosed political reasoning that is resigned to the harsh reality of violence and that barters over its incremental degrees. Resilience is Thatcherite *Realpolitik* of the toughest kind. Taking for granted that there is no such thing as society, it regards damage and violence as individual dramas, requiring individual solutions.

In contemporary disaster studies, resilience is an absolute buzzword. A Google Scholar search on 'disaster' and 'resilience' brings up the following examples in 0.2 seconds. *Designing Resilience: Preparing for Extreme Events* (Comfort, Boin et al., 2010), 'Psychological Resilience After Disaster. New York City in the Aftermath of the September 11th Terrorist Attack' (Bonanno, Galea et al., 2006), *The Resilience Dividend: Being Strong in a World where Things go Wrong* (Rodin, 2014) and *Women Confronting Natural Disaster. From Vulnerability to Resilience* (Enarson, 2012). Schematically, these works all present the same basic argument, split into five parts. 1) A hazard or source of harm is diagnosed; 2) It is noted that marginalised groups (poor people, people of colour, women, children etc.) are disproportionately vulnerable to this natural or man-made hazard; 3) Vulnerable groups' self-help practices are studied that show how strong communities recover from their incurred damage and rise above their woeful predicament; 4) It is concluded that some communities are more resilient in overcoming their damage than others; 5) Those successful communities are rewarded through capital or status gains, while those who are insufficiently resilient are stigmatised as underperforming.

The problem with this argument is that it focuses on a community's resilient capacities, thus naturalising the damage incurred, which is presented as unavoidable. In the words of disaster researcher Kathleen Tierney, in resilience, 'disruptive change is naturalised and framed as inevitable. Its root causes cannot be altered, and the only reasonable response is to adapt' (2015:1333). This fatalism is captured by what cultural theorist Robin James calls the resilience cycle. Firstly, damage is incited (disaster strikes due to vulnerable conditions). Secondly, that damage is 'spectacularly overcome and that overcoming is broadcast' (2015:7). Thirdly, those who overcome are rewarded with status or capital gains, while those who do not manage to overcome are shamed as failures to 'normal' ways of coping with stress. As Robin James concludes:

Resilience is [. . .] the underlying value or ideal that determines how we organize [. . .] political and social institutions, the economy, concepts of selfhood, and so on. Resilience is the hegemonic or 'common sense' ideology that everything is to be measured [. . .] by its health. This 'health' is maintained by bouncing back from injury and crisis in a way that capitalizes on deficits so that you end up ahead of where you initially started (one step back, two steps forward). (2015:4)

The irony is that even though disaster studies champions resilience to overcome structural vulnerability, it is absurd to presume resilience could do so in the long run. Resilience needs damage to thrive, since without it, the task of overcoming would be impossible, and its connected capital and status gains would be annulled. While I agree with vulnerability studies' critical investigations into structural exposure to harm, I reject its premise that communities are best served by becoming resilient to their predicament. Resilience appears as the wrong answer to a correct question.

I argue that the fundamental disregard for African American lives that the US government demonstrated by letting disaster victims rot in the streets of New Orleans alerts us to a dimension of disaster that vulnerability studies does not capture, since it happens at a remove from a direct hazard. While vulnerability studies may analyse the disproportionate vulnerability of blacks during Hurricane Katrina, which it has variously attributed to disaster myths and racist media bias (Tierney, 2006) the absence of car ownership for the evacuation of the black community (Litman, 2006) or problems in elder care (Brunkard, Namulanda et al., 2008) it cannot account for the fact that despite desegregation and the gains of the Civil Rights Movement, since the 1960s, blacks have had a life expectancy that has consistently been between four to ten years lower than that of white people (Keith and Smith, 1988:625; *Economist*, 2019: para. 6). To account for this persistent racial disadvantage, we need to look at how systems of domination are reproduced through the slow, biopolitical rhythms of social reproduction.

3

Disasters and Social Reproduction

From the Italian pirates of the eleventh century to the slave labour in the Dominican Republic or Brazil today, capitalism has never stopped its 'looting' of labour power and resources 'outside' the closed system of exchange of equivalents.

— Loren Goldner

DISASTER AS A CRISIS OF REPRODUCTION

When crossing the narrow bridge on St. Claude Avenue that connects the heavily gentrified Bywater area with the Lower Ninth Ward, the sensation is one of travelling in time. While slightly further upstream on the Mississippi, towards the Old Town and the French Quarter, package tourists mingle with hipsters who have moved to the Bywater from Brooklyn for the low rent, the Lower Ninth Ward appears almost depopulated. Going north on Flood St, away from the levee that delimits the Mississippi, approximately every second house is boarded up and abandoned. Interspersed in between are stubborn residents who have returned to their destroyed neighbourhood. They appear at once lonely and defiant, like the last people on Earth. Further on, the houses become increasingly sparse and empty lots take over until the built environment stops entirely. From then on, it's just acres and acres of wilderness. In the area worst hit by Hurricane Katrina, every house was washed away, as the dilapidated levee system failed, and the water of Lake Pontchartrain inundated the low-lying parts of the city.

Even before Katrina, the Lower Ninth Ward and neighbouring St. Bernard Parish were regularly flooded. Naturally vulnerable to flooding due to its low-lying position, this area has been made more vulnerable still through the construction of a canal network, meant to facilitate shipping on the Mississippi, that eradicated much of the swamp and marshland that had served as natural flood protection. On the way back onto higher ground, rows of IKEA-style houses look like prefabs from an architecture catalogue. They are in stark contrast to the surrounding modest wooden houses, which is not surprising, since Brad Pitt's *Make It Right Foundation* built them. The intention was to provide affordable, ecological and energy-friendly housing for residents who had lost their homes. However, the houses go for three times the price of a normal Lower Ninth Ward house.

In the cartography of contemporary disaster politics, the Lower Ninth Ward is a complex nodal point, connecting contempt for the poor with environmental violence, structural racism and the capitalism of reconstruction. Despite its complexity, we can see that at the very basic level, Katrina represents a problem for social reproduction, defined as the ability of people to maintain their lives and livelihoods on a daily basis. It is curious that, while constantly addressing reproductive issues, disaster studies has so far not produced a systematic account of how disasters affect social reproduction and how the (mis)management of social reproduction results in disaster. As the historian Ted Steinberg remarks: 'There is much to be learned [. . .] by studying the history of natural disasters from the vantage point of political economy, especially given how little serious attention has been devoted to the topic' (2000:xvi).

SOCIAL REPRODUCTION THEORY

With such a commitment at heart, this book develops a social reproduction approach to disasters. Social reproduction theory emerged from within strands of Marxist Feminist social science in the 1960s and 1970s. Nuancing the orthodox Marxist insistence on wage labour, social reproduction theorists argued that the sphere of salaried commodity production necessitated another sphere, in which the workers and their labour power were reconstituted on a daily basis. While this reproductive sphere had been sidelined by Marxist and non-Marxist accounts of capitalist development on account of it being 'unproductive' and often unwaged, social reproduction theorists argued that it constituted an integral part of society's overall process of wealth production. As a consequence, Marxist feminism extended the critical gaze to the historical role of women in the reproduction of labour power through housework, the care for non-workers like children or the elderly, and the production of fresh workers through childbirth (Dalla Costa and James, 1975; James, 1976; Federici, 2012).

At the beginning of theories of social reproduction lies Karl Marx's materialist belief that it is the 'embodied human practices through which socio-material life is produced and reproduced' (Ferguson and McNally, 2013:xviii). Consider how Marx frames the relation between production and reproduction in *Capital*. In Marx's discussion of the capitalist mode of production, what is concretely produced are commodities and what is concretely reproduced is labour power. In fact, the two encounter each other in the commodity, since for Marx, what appears as the natural realm of commodity circulation in fact masks the commodities' point of origin in the dead labour that lies congealed in them. For Marx and in line with his epoch's fascination with productive work, it is thus human labour power that forms the basis of any productive system – as it essentially pertains to all humans – irrespective of their historical mode of production:

> We mean by labour-power, or labour-capacity, the aggregate of those mental and physical capabilities existing in the physical form, the living personality, of a human being, capabilities which he sets in motion whenever he produces a use-value of any kind [. . .] Labour, then, as the creator of use-values, as useful labour, is a condition of human existence which is independent of all forms of society. It is an eternal natural necessity which mediates the metabolism between man and nature, and therefore human life itself. (1976:270,133)

For Marx, labour power is the capacity to expend energy to extract a simple use out of any object, activity or process. As such, it forms the basis for capitalist production or any other social production process. If labour power is the potential to perform labour, then it is actualised in the labouring activity itself. 'Labour power in use is labour itself' (ibid.:173), as Marx confirms. Labour then is intimately tied to the living body of the worker, but it also necessarily encompasses a social component, as for Marx, labour is never isolated but always occurs within a socially defined mode of production. In this dual definition of labour as both biological and social lies the crux of Marx's understanding of how society is reproduced. In order for any economic system to survive, society must reproduce a sufficient number of workers to continue the labour process. In addition, however, it must also reproduce the social conditions necessary for new workers to enter the labour force effectively. These social components include, for example, institutions, administrative structures and regulatory mechanisms. Marx gives the example of feudal society, in which 'the product of the serf must [. . .] suffice to reproduce his *conditions of labour*, in addition to his subsistence' (ibid.:531 Emphasis mine).

While Marx elaborated on the social component of reproduction in his discussions of the state and of ideology, he doesn't dwell on the biological side of reproduction at any particular length. Claiming that the labour power that workers sell on the market is 'not a commodity like any other, for it is not produced capitalistically' (Vogel, 2013:157), Marx seems to argue that labour power is 'naturally' reproduced by kinship structures such as the family that themselves pre-exist the development of capitalism. Marx thus envisions capitalism as simply latching on to a kinship system that itself is left unchanged by it. In *Capital* he writes:

> The maintenance and reproduction of the working class remains a necessary condition for the reproduction of capital. But the capitalist may safely leave this to the worker's drives for self-preservation and propagation. All the capitalist cares for is to reduce the worker's individual consumption to the necessary minimum. (1976:718)

What Marx here naturalises is the domestic sphere of the home and the housework that is daily performed in it. With this oversight, he also neglected the gendered dimension of this particular kind of reproductive work that is still today predominantly done by women. Indeed, Marx's anthropology presumed a cyclical and primitive reproduction to naturally occur in any given social system as an anthropological constant:

> Whatever the form of the process of production in a society, it must be a continuous process, must continue to go periodically through the same phases. A society can no more cease to produce than it can cease to consume. When viewed, therefore, as a connected whole, and as flowing on with incessant renewal, every social process of production is, at the same time, a process of reproduction. (1975:565)

In opposition to this view of social reproduction as natural, organic and biologically determined, Marxist feminists in the 1970s began to theorise reproduction as the disavowed social relation at the heart of society. The group Wages for Housework (WfH) is exemplary in this regard. Founded by the socialist feminists Silvia Federici, Mariarosa Dalla Costa, Selma James and Brigitte Galtier, WfH's basic claim was that Marx and the bulk of Marxist theory after him had grossly neglected the sphere of domestic work or housework that was the condition of possibility for the capitalist economy. They argued that the sphere of social reproduction, encompassing domestic work, childcare and elder care was excluded from consideration by the focus on productive work that privileged value-producing activities, mainly carried out by men. In the words of Silvia Federici: 'The reproduction of human beings is the foundation of every economic and political system, and [. . .] the immense amount of paid and unpaid domestic work done by women in the home is what keeps the world moving' (2012:2).

In straight continuation with Marx, what was concretely meant by reproduction was the reproduction of labour power or the maintenance, care and reconstitution of bodies with the ability to work. In the post-WWII era, women in the home mostly carried out this type of domestic work and feminists attempted to frame their experience through the concepts of Marxian political economy. In this way, the mundane chores of cooking, cleaning and childcare as well as the sexual politics of the bedroom came under critical scrutiny. While Marx recognised that during labour 'a definite quantity of human muscle, nerve, brain, &c., is wasted, and these require to be restored' (1975:181), his subsequent discussion centres on the wage, necessary to ensure this daily restoration and not on the unwaged domestic labour that ensures the worker's physical and emotional recovery, entirely outside the wage relation. Recognising Marx's gender blindness, one of the central aims of WfH was to gain a clearer analytical grasp on the precise nature of housework and its value within a Marxist framework.

However, besides a conceptual engagement with Marxist theory, WfH also developed a distinct political presence. Its strategy was to demand a wage for its performance of housework in order to denaturalise domestic labour and force its recognition as socially necessary work. WfH argued that domestic labour was both productive of labour power as well as directly productive of capital and should therefore be adequately remunerated. Using the Italian autonomist Mario Tronti's concept of the 'social factory' (Tronti, 2019), to capture the subsumption of formerly unproductive spheres of life by the capitalist profit motive, women's reproductive labour in the home was recast as a foundational form of directly productive activity. Contrary to the established Marxist understanding, housework was not the 'other' of factory production, but instead itself a central production site.

WfH was practically inspired by the American Welfare Mothers' initiative that saw black, female welfare recipients demand a wage for the raising of their children, rather than asking to be put to work. For WfH, the artificial division of the working class into men, who earned a wage in the factory, and women who restored them physically and mentally after work, was intended to separate the proletariat into wage-earners on the one hand and a naturalised sphere of reproductive work on the other that was framed as a 'labour of love'. WfH posited that capitalism used the wage instrumentally to naturalise those types of work that were vital to its functioning but not acknowledged into the production process:

> WfH was a revolutionary perspective not only because it exposed the root cause of 'women's oppression' in a capitalist society but because it unmasked the main mechanisms by which capitalism has maintained its power and kept the working class divided. These are the devaluation of entire spheres of human activity [. . .] and the ability to [. . .] extract work also from a large population of workers [. . .] outside the wage relation: slaves, colonial subjects, prisoners, housewives, and students [. . .] WfH was revolutionary [. . .] because we recognized that capitalism requires unwaged reproductive labor in order to contain the cost of labor power, and we believed that a successful campaign draining the source of this unpaid labor would break the process of capital accumulation. (Federici, 2012:8–9)

In the 1970s, at a time when the international women's movement focused on getting women out of the home and into the workplace, many feminists did not view WfH favourably.[14] However, it is important to note the double strategy in the claim of wages for housework. As Federici emphasised, the demand for wages *for* housework was at the same time a demand for wages *against* housework, since the campaigning women knew that it was structurally impossible for capitalism to pay housewives adequately for their labour. There was thus a strong performative dimension to their demand that aimed to demonstrate precisely the incapacity of the capitalist system to remunerate all of its workers equally for their labour. In this sense, WfH was much more radical than the mainstream feminists' demand of integration into the workplace, since it aimed to show the limits of the wage to ever provide more just and equal social relations. Capitalism, WfH argued, rested entirely on certain types of reproductive labour that were being made structurally non-labour.[15]

A DIALECTIC OF SOCIAL SPHERES

This emphasis on the structural relation between a productive sphere that is officially validated as such and a reproductive sphere, whose social function is framed as a 'labour of love' is key to my understanding of disaster. While state-led disaster relief is officially validated labour, carried out by salaried aid workers, community-run disaster relief is carried out for free by families, neighbours and the community. In their analysis of the reproductive process, the political theorists Maya Gonzales and Jeanne Neton have systematised this relation in a way that contributes greatly to our discussion by offering a set of binary relations. The first binary exists between the commercial sector where activities are performed for a direct profit and the non-commercial sector where activities are performed at a remove from immediate market interest. Gonzales and Neton call these spheres 'directly market-mediated' (DMM), and 'indirectly market-mediated' (IMM) to highlight their interconnectedness in the totality of the capitalist mode of production (2014:153). In the decades preceding the neoliberal turn of the 1970s, disaster aid, along with other public services has been firmly on the side of the IMM sphere, existing as a state-run investment into the reproduction of the population.

The second binary exists between waged and unwaged forms of activity that don't necessarily overlap with the commercial and non-commercial spheres. Importantly for our case, and as Gonzales and Neton emphasise, many reproductive services like education, health care and disaster aid are clearly not-for-profit activities and therefore unproductive of value. However, since they are performed by civil servants or salaried employees, they still constitute a socially recognised form of labour, the cost of which is paid for indirectly through deductions from collective taxes. They thus form paid, non-commercial IMM activities. By contrast, voluntary, unpaid disaster aid constitutes non-waged, non-commercial work. It therefore strictly speaking does not represent labour but a kind of extra-activity, usually grounded in an affective motive, such as goodwill, love or charity. Gonzales and Neton call this the sphere of 'unwaged indirect market mediation' (2014:170). It is important to recognise how, even if – from the perspective of the market – they are structurally non-labour, these types of activity nevertheless form a large part of the reproduction of capitalist economic and political relations.

While formerly in the sphere of waged IMM activities, the US state has been increasingly unwilling to provide the public service of disaster aid. In the United States, budgets have been significantly cut, despite an increasing disaster rate. Some of these erstwhile state-run services were privatised and transformed into commercial DMM activities in the form of insurances, thereby maintaining their relationship to the wage, while a large part of them stayed in the IMM sphere but became the unwaged responsibility of volunteers. Gonzeles and Neton have a specific name for this dynamic in which formerly state-run IMM activities are cut and foisted back onto communities because they are seen as too costly. They call this 'the process of abjection' to denote the sloughing off of reproductive activities from the formally recognised IMM and DMM spheres onto the community:

> Indeed, the category of the abject refers specifically to activities that became waged at some point but are in the process of returning into the unwaged IMM sphere because they've become too costly for the state or capital [. . .] These will become DMM for those who can afford it (privatization) or lapse into the sphere of unwaged indirect market mediation. (2014:170–71)

While the process of abjection adds a dynamism to Gonzales and Neton's otherwise static terminology, it is important to point out that all social spheres may (and have been) involved in social reproduction. Indeed, social reproduction has historically moved fluidly between the IMM, DMM and abject spheres. Understanding this is vital, if we want to criticise disaster studies' fixed understanding of the actors involved in disasters. Research into disasters and disaster interventions traditionally focus on two categories of actors: large-scale and formal actors, such as humanitarian organisations, stately and supra-stately institutions on the one hand, and individuals in and around the disaster area, defined either as victims or volunteers, on the other. This division matches the classical division of social life into a public sphere, occupied by the state, the media and individuals defined as citizens and a private sphere, occupied by individuals as their informal, domestic selves.[16] Indeed, in the US, the history of federal disaster relief to this day can be narrated as the on-going negotiation of the fraught division between the public and the private (Moss, 1999).

The perspective of social reproduction on the other hand teaches us that both the state, and civil society are historically constituted entities. Indeed, civil society itself is generated only through repeated acts of social reproductive labour. This labour can be carried out by the state, by the market or by social actors, such as families and communities. The overall process of social reproduction can therefore be differentiated into state-led, market-led and civil society-led forms that have taken different shapes across history. The advantage of this perspective, which looks at social reproduction as the way in which bodies and minds are replenished under capitalism, is that it takes a specific labour-approach to disasters, in which activities as diverse as rescue operations, care work and food provision are seen as distinct areas of work that are necessary for the workforce to be reconstituted, and whose chores are unequally distributed across the population. It thus allows a socio-materialist analysis of the forms of disaster relief that are normally passed off as acts of altruism or goodwill and instead allows them to be seen as abject; as activities that the state formerly performed but has become unwilling to do.

4

1930: Disasters, Natural and Federal

It is simply indescribably beautiful here – the way one always imagines
the Riviera, and the way it never actually is.

— Theodor W. Adorno

THE ECONOMIC EMERGENCY

To begin to understand the contemporary shift of disaster relief from
the waged IMM to the abject sphere, it is important to cast a glance onto
the history of US disaster relief in the early twentieth century, before
the advent of the 1970s economic crisis, in a different age of boom and
bust. How did disaster relief become integrated into the repertoire of
waged IMM activities in the first place and what purpose did this integration serve? After all, in the nineteenth century, the idea that a strong
federal government should provide emergency relief for its people would
have seemed fantastical. Taking hurricane reconstruction in the state of
Florida as an example, this chapter examines the way in which disaster
relief shifted from individual state to federal responsibility under the
New Deal and during the post-war boom.

I argue that moving disaster aid from the municipal into the federal
realm served two key purposes: On the one hand, it created ample
opportunities for employment in an ailing economic environment. On
the other hand, it allowed for the extension of infrastructure and real
estate development to formerly inaccessible regions of the nation, setting
off a colossal development boom. The short-lived presence of a strong
quasi social-democratic government informed the idea of a compromise
between the newly constituted working class and the federal state, cul-
minating in the conviction that the advance of capitalist development
was beneficial for organised labour. Disaster aid was thus instrumental
in reconfiguring the relationship between the state and civil society as a
union of shared interests. In the following chapters, we will see how this
partnership quickly disintegrated with the advent of the 1970s crisis.

In 1934 the small island of Key West on the southernmost tip of Florida was knee-deep in depression. With some 80 per cent of its 11,600 citizens on welfare benefits, Governor David Sholtz resorted to unprecedented action. On 2 July, he declared a state of emergency in Key West and handed all administrative powers to the federal government. In response, Julius F. Stone, a convinced New Dealer and head of the Federal Emergency Relief Administration (FERA) – a forerunner of today's FEMA – set up shop in Key West and began reshaping the destiny of southern Florida. Faced with the choice of relocating the roughly 3,000 local families to other parts of the state or providing a large cash donation as poverty relief, he instead decided to put the unemployed Key West residents to work and re-establish their ailing town as a number one tourist resort.

In the following months, Key West became the poster child of the American New Deal and living proof of the credo that injecting poverty-stricken areas with generous federal relief could bring stalling economies back onto their feet. Volunteers from across the nation flooded into the area and together with local residents and $1 billion in emergency budgets, razed derelict buildings to make way for attractive cabanas, renovated parks, planted palm trees and flower beds and restored the city's characteristic architecture. The FERA publicist M. E. Golfond advertised the reconstruction effort to national media and the city quickly reaped the publicity campaign's benefits. As tourist season came around, 40,000 holidaymakers with federally subsidised airfares and ferry rates descended on Key West,[17] forcing more established residents like Ernest Hemingway to flee his 'St. Tropez of the poor' and resettle in Cuba.

THE PUBLIC-PRIVATE PARTNERSHIP:
DISASTER AID AND DEVELOPMENT

Florida was not always the sunshine paradise that it represents today. In the nineteenth century, its main – and modest – income came from tobacco plantations, citrus fruit and other types of tropical agriculture (Revels, 2011:13). The first visitors to Florida did not come for pleasure but to inhale the state's supposedly salubrious air, said to alleviate the symptoms of tuberculosis (Stronge, 2008:77–8). According to historian Tracy Revels, early Florida tourism at the turn of the century lived mainly off of the state's reputation for healthy air and clean waters, combined with sporting activities like swimming, fishing or hunting. When the new-built Orange Belt railroad made St. Petersburg on the Gulf Coast widely accessible, the town became the state's first major recreational destination, where well-off Midwesterners travelled to enjoy the alleged health benefits of the mild climate (Revels, 2011:106).

While political theory insists on a rigid distinction between the state sector and the private sector, in the early twentieth century, federal involvement often went hand in hand with corporate interests, as state-planned infrastructure was frequently carried out by corporate sub-contractors. The development of Florida is a case in point for these early public private partnerships. Florida experienced the first large extension of its road and highway network between 1911 and 1921, courtesy of the federal government's Road Act (1916) and Highway Act (1921). Well-paved highways, connecting Jacksonville and Miami as well as roads linking the Gulf and the Atlantic Coasts brought Florida its first tourism boom in the early 1920s. Particularly the Dixie Highway that connected Florida to Chicago and the Tamami Trail that accessed the Everglades from Miami and Ft. Myers, provided a fresh influx of visitors from the north, peaking at 2.5 million tourists a year in 1925 (Revels, 2011:109).

Observing the rapid, state-funded development of the Gulf Coast, the railway tycoons Henry Flagler and Henry Plant began extending the Florida railroad network to access the difficult-to-reach southern and eastern parts of the state. Following the increase in infrastructural development, Flagler and Plant also began building hotels and resorts to cater to the tourists they themselves brought in on their railroads in an early example of vertically integrated service provision. Even if the tourism industry emphasised the 'natural' beauty of the Sunshine State, already by 1920, much of the Florida landscape had been engineered to fit the tourist taste. Miami Beach for instance was created in the summer of 1913, when an investor dredged 1,000 acres of mangrove swamp and shipped in six million cubic yards of soil from the Everglades to smooth over the coast and create a white, sandy beach. As the historian Polly Redford writes in *Billon-Dollar Sandbar: A Biography of Miami Beach*, whose title announces a curious meshing of personhood and nature: 'The original landscape was erased as if it had never been and a more salable one built in its place' (1970:73).

Fellow historian Ted Steinberg further outlines how publicly owned coastal areas were gradually sold off to private investors, beginning in the late nineteenth century (2000:49). By the early twentieth century, the private acquisition of oceanfront property combined with modern technologies of reclaiming marshland through dredging and landfill spurred a real estate boom around coastal properties in Florida, as hotel developers offered ever higher prices for a piece of the tourism pie. In 1925, Carl Fisher, the developer and creator of Miami Beach, sold properties totalling 23 million US dollars in just one year (ibid.). However, in the early twentieth century, the infrastructure boom wasn't restricted to the Sunshine State alone. Road and rail networks were expanding all across the country. We have to contextualise Florida's development in the 1920s within the nationwide extension of infrastructure to get a more thorough view of the expansion of state-led social reproduction in its historical significance.

Let us first ask in what way we can understand infrastructure development as state-led social reproduction. Theoretically, and in keeping with the division of social activity under capitalism into a for-profit (DMM) sphere and a non-profit (IMM) sphere, infrastructural expansion – such as the building of roads and railways – can be carried out in either sphere. While Florida's railway network was built by Flagler and Plant's for-profit private construction companies, much infrastructural development in the early twentieth century was realised by the state, rather than by commercial operators. Funded by taxpayers' money, public construction took place in the waged IMM sphere, at a remove from direct profit-making. However, this type of construction was never separate from the market, as facilitating access to previously isolated areas also created new business opportunities for capital. Like most state-led social reproduction, infrastructural expansion is thus indirectly market-mediated, providing employment for the population, while also furthering economic interests for capitalist profit-making. We will see how, particularly in Florida and California, the economic aspect of infrastructural development gradually supplanted its public role, as tourism and hotel operators lobbied for state support to develop these hazard-prone regions.[18]

INFRASTRUCTURE, LABOUR AND THE STATE

Infrastructural development played a pivotal role in the process of American industrialisation in the late nineteenth and early twentieth century. Indeed, the spread of Fordist factory production would have been unthinkable without the network of roads, highways and freeways that connected distant cities to each other and made remote areas accessible for development. At the same time as the federal state was expanding its reach to evermore far-flung locations, the wave of infrastructural development set the stage for the brief ascent of organised labour as a driving political force in American everyday life. Pivotal for this dual trajectory was the departure from a liberal laissez-faire economy that was replaced with the model of a strong state that acted as investor, planner and employer all at once. The research group Endnotes emphasise that in the late nineteenth century:

> Many states dropped pretenses to *Manchestertum*; they began to intervene extensively in national economies. That they did so made it possible to build a vast infrastructure, on which the new industries ran. Here were the canals, railroads and telegraph wires; here, too, the roads, telephone wires, gas lines, plumbing, and electrical grids. At first, this infrastructure was one dimensional: railroads and canals cut through the landscape. Then, it became increasingly two (or even three) dimensional: networks of roads, electrical grids and radio towers covered entire areas. (2015b:109)

As we have seen in the construction of the railway network in Florida, private corporations alone did not have the capacities, skills or funds to carry out these nationwide projects. Because of this, the federal state became a kind of master-administrator, employing specialist urban planners and architects to lay the foundations for a new and interconnected type of society that had hitherto been primarily locally organised. Endnotes specifies that:

> This sort of undertaking was often too difficult for capitalists, and not only because of the huge scale of investment required. To build a massive infrastructure requires an army of planners: to promote a wide reach, to prevent wasteful duplication and to decide on industry standards. That meant a growing role for the state, as the only part of society capable of becoming adequate to this task — the task of planning society. (2015b:109–10)

However, by placing such great emphasis on the state as the main construction overseer, Endnotes neglects the extent to which infrastructure projects in the US often ran as early public-private partnerships, with the state as planner and developer, who then subcontracted the construction to private corporations. The scale of these projects is staggering, even from today's perspective. By the turn of the century, the US had built a railway network spanning 200,000 miles across the whole North American continent (Easterling, 2014:152). The extent of these operations meant a huge demand for labour. Besides a war economy where workers are being massively employed in arms manufacturing, infrastructure development requires the highest possible amount of manual labour. The economic historian Alfred Chandler has captured the monstrous reach of the corporations that carried out the construction of the American railroad network:

> For several decades the consolidated US railroad systems remained the largest business enterprise in the world [. . .] In the 1890s a single railroad system managed more men and handled more funds and transactions and used more capital than the most complex of American governmental and military organizations. In 1891 the Pennsylvania Railroad employed over 100,000 workers. In the same year, the total number of soldiers, sailors, and marines in the United States armed services was 39,492. (1977:94, 204–5)

The new role of the federal state as general planner and mass employer changed previous leftist ideas regarding the handling of this huge bureaucratic formation. Not only did it seem rational that only a strong federal state was able to carry out infrastructure programmes of such magnitude, workers also benefitted directly from these operations because they provided them with the perspective of full employment. This meant that Marx's doctrine that after a revolutionary takeover, the state would simply 'wither away', began to look increasingly unlikely. Instead, the idea of socialism as the ultimate planning of society emerged, in which a strong state would administer the workers' interests without regard for the gains of big business and capital. As Endnotes specifies, 'Socialism became a vision of the endless extension of the state – from partially to totally planned society' (2015b:111).

For a while, this horizon seemed a possibility. The massive need for labour in key industrial and infrastructural industries swelled the ranks of the unions and in turn created political leverage for wage and benefit negotiations. The consensus was that workers were never better off than under highly developed capitalism. Socialism would therefore have to adopt full industrialisation and full employment as its doctrines of choice, creating a world much like capitalism, but with a different set of administrators. In this way, the hitherto endorsed prospect of communism as the abolition of capital *and* the state retreated into the background and was replaced by social democracy, encapsulated in the idea of an electoral takeover of the state. Backed by strong workers' unions and active in most national parliaments in Europe and North America, social democrats in the early twentieth century endorsed the general direction of industrialisation, but sought to institute reforms that would make the lives of workers more palatable. As the historian Adam Przeworski writes of social democratic parties in the 1920s:

> If socialists could not pursue an immediate program of nationaliza-
> tion, what could they do in the meantime? They could and did pursue
> ad-hoc measures designed to improve the conditions of workers:
> develop housing programs, introduce minimal wage laws, institute
> some protection from unemployment [. . .] Such measures, although
> they favoured workers, were neither politically unfeasible nor eco-
> nomically shocking – they continued the tradition of the reforms of
> Bismarck, Disraeli, and Giolitti. These measures modified neither the
> structure of the economy nor the political balance of forces. (1985:35)

The development of southern Florida and the commercial provision of tourist activities embody capital and labour's shared dream of indus-trial progress. Indeed, boosting the economy of the Sunshine State was a double boon for the federal government *and* parts of the working and growing middle classes. During the 1920s, it provided ample industrial employment in a formerly underdeveloped agricultural region. At the same time, the short-lived economic boom of the twenties saw a rise in real wages and a reduction in working hours for industrial workers, which for the first time instilled the bourgeois idea of the family vacation in the minds of the working class. Simultaneously, the development of Henry Ford's Model T car ensured that workers could spend their extra income on increasing their mobility and going on holiday, independently of ticket prices and train schedules. As Tracy Revels writes:

> People had more leisure time than ever before; even industrial workers
> were beginning to receive regular vacations. As hours declined,
> wages rose and by the 1920s [. . .] the average American's income was
> approximately twice what he or she needed to meet the basic neces-

sities of life [. . .] With the automobile came a sense of wanderlust, as thousands of people who had never before travelled took to the road. (2011:103,108)

In the early 1920s, the Miami Chamber of Commerce officially launched a nationwide billboard campaign that advertised Florida's endless summer to frostbitten city-dwellers in the north: 'It's always June in Miami', billboards from Chicago to New York read, with scantily clad Southern Belles driving the point to its northern home.[19]

1920S HURRICANE SEASON

'Like a vacation, the Florida boom was exciting, memorable and short-lived' (2011:122), writes Tracy Revels of the beginning of the 1920s hurricane season. On 18 September 1926, the strongest hurricane in Weather Bureau history destroyed much of Florida's precarious coastal development. A storm surge of more than 15 feet washed away hotels, destroyed boats, left hundreds dead and created property damage of over $112 million (ibid.). While the dredging of natural mangrove swamp and the rampant development of seaside properties was arguably good for business, it also destroyed the coast's natural protection against hurricane-induced storm surges. Florida's boosters had taken no precautions against the possibility of hurricanes and their hotels, casinos and resorts – built directly on the beach – did not withstand the winds. Almost two years later on the dot, in September 1928, another category four storm crashed into West Palm Beach, bringing torrential rainfall that flooded the large inland areas around Lake Okeechobee. In a ghostly foreshadowing of Hurricane Katrina, families were stranded on their rooftops or simply washed away by the rising tide. Over 3,500 people never returned home and 'the image of bloated bodies, piled like cordwood was a sharp contrast, and a bitter finale, to the scenes of beachfront idylls and freewheeling speculation that had defined Florida in the 1920s' (ibid.:123).

However, the 1920s tourism finale was not so final after all. When the economic depression added to Florida's misery by also putting those not employed in tourism out of work, the federal government, now under the New Deal, stepped in to rebuild large parts of the destroyed infrastructure. The Works Progress Administration (WPA) and the Civilian Conservation Corps (CCC) rebuilt parks, airports, campgrounds and roads and federal money was used to re-establish the hard-hit Key West as a tourist resort. This extensive investment by the federal government into Florida's tourism sector became one of the staples of Roosevelt's New Deal. It also made Miami the first city to officially exit the Great Depression in 1935 (Revels, 2011:131).

Confronted with a seminal economic crisis, the New Dealers shouldered the cost of social reproduction by treating the crisis like a natural disaster, in which the needy deserved relief. The legal scholar Michele Dauber has traced the way in which, under the New Deal, poverty was framed as a contingent 'natural' disaster, rather than as a systemic crisis of capital accumulation (Dauber, 2013:79–127). The tactic was successful and poverty-stricken areas received generous federal support under the banner of emergency relief. In the early 1930s, the first nationwide relief initiative, launched through the Federal Emergency Relief Act (FERA) began to extend its charitable support for children, the disabled and widows to the unemployed in general. In addition, the 1940s witnessed a wider shift in the way that disaster relief was administered. Its provision migrated from being a state-run and *ad hoc* operation, to being a key federal responsibility. This allowed the government to influence much more directly the manner in which relief operations were carried out. It also crucially shifted the budgetary burden from local residents to taxpayers nationwide.

However, it would be misguided to see the vast extension of state-led social reproduction under the New Deal as anything but capitalist. In the eyes of the New Dealers, the Great Depression had highlighted the dangers of too much free-floating capital. Without new possibilities for investment, markets had tumbled into an epochal crisis from which the world was still reeling. Under the Roosevelt administration, the state intervened with massive spending programmes, employing workers to bring back buying power, expanding infrastructure to aid capitalist development, and giving out cheap loans to businesses. Rather than ushering in a post-capitalist future, the expansion of state-led social reproduction under the New Deal worked as a crisis fix to help the faltering economy back onto its feet and prevent the ripple effects of an economic downturn. As Ruth Wilson Gilmore highlights with regard to this type of disaster-socialism: 'Income and employment programs for workers, infrastructural programs for capital, and subsidy programs for farmlands were designed to keep surpluses from again accumulating into the broad and deep crisis that had characterized the Great Depression' (2007:79).

The expansion of infrastructural development is a case in point for the entwinement of directly and indirectly market-mediated social reproduction under capitalism, in which the state provides a taxpayer-funded safety blanket to investors. Fundamental to the New Deal's national operation to rebuild the economy was the development of a public works programme, in which large infrastructure projects were commissioned and overseen by the federal state and carried out by corporate subcontractors. Assisted by the federal government, developers in the 1940s built entire new towns on reclaimed land by dredging coastal lands that were in reality not more than swamp and marsh. Ted Steinberg has outlined how 'developers discovered the extreme marketability of dredge-filled marsh, popular among prospective homeowners seeking easy water access for their boats' (2000:83).

The state sponsored the operation by constructing bridges, roads and paved streets, accessing the new landmass and enabling a steady influx of fresh tourists, eager to spend their extra cash on a sunshine vacation after the austere and restrained wartime years. But not everyone who came also left. In the decade from 1950 to 1960, the population of the Florida Keys tripled (Steinberg, 2000:85), as federally sponsored roads made Florida's southernmost tip widely accessible. Ted Steinberg confirms that:

> The federal government [. . .] proved itself a zealous supporter of life by the sea. Beginning in the 1930s and accelerating after the Second World War, the US government subsidized land use on barrier islands by helping bear the costs of constructing causeways, bridges and water supply systems, in addition to providing disaster relief. In response, land speculation and population growth reached new heights. (2000:85)

FROM PROLETARIAT TO PEOPLE'S PARTY

This extension of state-led social reproduction under the banner of disaster meant that after the war, working class parties were forced to reconsider their tactics. The envisioned parliamentary victory had not come to pass. In no country did working class parties ever secure an absolute majority. The dilemma was that once socialists had embraced the parliamentary system in the hope of one day taking over the government, they were bound by that system and condemned to the teleological hope of the rational advance of the socialisation of labour. On the one hand, as industrialisation and the extension of large-scale infrastructure projects continued undamped after the war, this aim seemed more attainable by the year. At the same time, it appeared illogical that the extension of organised labour did not lead to electoral victory or bring closer the abolition of capitalist labour relations. The truth is that class seemed like a remote identificatory container for people who often still identified along race and gender, or skill and religious lines. Przeworski confirms that particularly at a time of economic prosperity: 'Socialism seemed an abstract and an alien ideology in relation to daily experience. It was not apparent to workers that an improvement of their conditions required that the very system of wage labour must be abolished' (1985:22).

Because its goals seemed unrealistic, socialism was a hard sell for the electorate. Furthermore, socialist parties had extreme race and gender reservations, championing the white, male factory worker as their ideal and ignoring the huge amounts of informal or domestic labour carried out by women and people of colour. The thinness of their own electoral base meant that socialist parties had to look for alliances with broader segments of the population outside of their immediate class base. This explains the diffusion of working-class politics into the wider reaches of the popular parties or people's parties after the Second World War. The only way for working class parties to gain parliamentary power was to not *only* campaign for direct workers' interests but to extend their political constituency by addressing issues that were of wider social relevance or ran tangential to workers' concerns.

These newly endorsed policies had to be policies that many people could agree on. Classically, they followed campaigns for the extension of state-led social reproduction, including reforms towards direct rather than indirect taxation, the redistributive extension of social spending towards education, pensions and health care, the facilitating of affordable public transport and housing. However, the adaptation of socialist ideas to a widely conceived politics of 'the people' also meant the jettisoning of class as a social determinant and conversely the abandonment of socialism as the overthrow of the parliamentary system. Przeworski argues that:

As class identification becomes less salient, socialist parties lose their unique appeal to workers. Social democratic parties are no longer qualitatively different from other parties; class loyalty is no longer the strongest base of self-identification. Workers see society as composed of individuals; they view themselves as members of collectivities other than class; they behave politically on the basis of religious, ethnic, regional, or some other affinity. (1985:28)

By creating abundant employment possibilities, the extension of infrastructure projects following natural disasters contributed to an extension of organised labour beyond the Marxist revolutionary model and towards the reformist model of Keynesianism. In this way, federal disaster relief and the centralisation of infrastructural planning created a shared dream of peaceful co-development between labour and capital, who would advance hand in hand into a bright future. Keynesianism was based on the idea that boosting the welfare of workers by extending state-led social reproduction through direct wage increases, as well as investing in other benefits such as a shorter work week, extended vacations and paid holidays would greatly benefit the economy by stimulating consumption. Rather than trying to abolish the state, as Marx had advised, Keynesianism suggested that socialist parties could use the state to impose reforms onto the free market to create a social market economy, in which the welfare of workers and business interests were reconciled in the prosperous consumer.

1960S HURRICANE SEASON

When the calm weather that followed the hurricanes of the 1920s came to a violent end in the early 1960s, all the necessary federal measures were already in place to restart Florida tourism without much disturbance to business as usual. A new law on emergency measures enabled the President to call a state of emergency and authorise the rebuilding of public infrastructure after a disaster without the necessity to seek approval by congress. In 1953, a law had been passed that granted the Small Business Administration (SBA) the powers to give out low-interest loans to house owners to build back after a disaster (Steinberg, 2000:86). As to the damage done to the beaches by hurricane-induced erosion, this was taken care of by Army Corps of Engineers' Beach Renourishment Program that shipped in sand and soil from the Everglades to replace the drastic loss of Miami Beach's sandy dunes, 'help wealthy hotel operators' (ibid.:81) and not upset the tourists.

Hurricanes Donna (1960), Cleo (1964) and Betsy (1965) could thus not do much to disrupt the endless summer of the Sunshine State. On the contrary, Ted Steinberg confirms that after Hurricane Donna: 'President Dwight Eisenhower declared the keys a disaster area following the storm, opening the way for millions of dollars to pour in to rebuild bridges, highways and water lines. The SBA meanwhile offered homeowners and businesses low-interest loans' (ibid.:86).

Due to the federalisation of disaster aid, poor taxpayers in Iowa or Kansas now bore the brunt of the reconstruction of Florida, a tourist paradise they would never set foot in. Furthermore, under Republican pressure, the provision of federal disaster relief was often offset with cuts to other social spending, particularly housing and health grants, devouring, in the words of urban theorist Mike Davis, 'a significant portion of what remain[ed] of discretionary spending' (1998:51). The federalisation of emergency budgets thus allowed the government to leverage diverse population needs against each other in a bargain for limited funds: If Floridian hotel operators received disaster relief, this now meant that school children 2000 miles away lost out on their teaching. In post-war Florida and California, the federalisation of emergency aid thus at times amounted to a redistribution of government money from poor to rich.[20] As Davis acerbically concludes: 'As if the poor do not already have enough to worry about, they now face the bizarre prospect that if Malibu burns or Hilton Head is blown away in a hurricane, they will have to foot the bill' (ibid.).

In the decades after WWII, the successful makeover of Key West thus became the template for a new type of disaster relief in Florida, only that this time, the calamity was natural rather than economic. In response to the hurricane wave of the 1960s, federal funds were poured into Florida by the millions to rebuild its destroyed tourist infrastructure, constituting one of the largest disaster aid programmes in US history. Indeed, tourism, both a social and an economic phenomenon, rose to unimaginable levels after WWII and quickly became a cultural fixture in the imaginary of the American bourgeoisie. In 1949, only four years after the end of the war, the US Department of Commerce established that 62% of all Americans were planning to take a holiday (Revels, 2011:157). A 1959 survey found that Florida received 11.3 million tourists each year, spending a total of $1.77 billion (ibid.:158). As publicity campaigns savvily advertised Florida as 'America's No. 1 tourist spot', its hotel tycoons boasted 'that since WWII, they had constructed more hotels than the rest of the world combined' (ibid.).

Yet, if the government's generosity helped Florida's economy to recover in the short-term, then its strategy of subsidising coastal development proved disastrous in the long term. As Florida entered a relatively calm period of hurricane activity after WWII and with tourist numbers restored to way above their 1920s peak, the speculative and dangerous business of coastal real estate development received a massive boost by continued federal investment into roads, bridges, water and sewage systems that 'placed more and more people in harm's way than ever before in the history of the Sunshine State' (Steinberg, 2000:80). As Steinberg further explains: 'The government's willingness to provide such money would turn out to be the start of a steady and monumental transfusion of federal cash for subsidising disaster vulnerability [. . .] In the postwar period, the federal government emerged as a major player in the political economy of risk' (ibid.).

TWO LIMITS TO CO-DEVELOPMENT

There was thus a natural and a social limit to the dream of peaceful co-development between capital and labour that had begun so hopefully in the early twentieth century. Regarding the natural limit, every generous rebuilding of infrastructure post-disaster escalated local communities' vulnerability by creating structures that were increasingly exposed to the vagaries of nature. The way in which disaster aid in Florida rendered undeveloped areas accessible to real estate boosters through the dredging of mangrove swamp and the renourishment of beaches was anathema to a sustained effort to diminish disaster vulnerability. Marxist ecologist James O'Connor (1998) calls this the 'second contradiction of capitalism', meaning a conflict between the development of the productive forces on the one hand and the coextensive exploitation of the environment on the other.

Sticking with O'Connor, we can define the social limit to the peaceful co-development between capital and labour as the first contradiction of capitalism, or the conflict between the extension of productive forces and the class relation. Against the dreams of Keynesianism, production did not continue infinitely along with rising wages and continued employment. Instead, beginning as early as 1960, the US economy went into an unchecked decline. Taking off in the late nineteenth century and buoyed by the war economies of armament and reconstruction, the US economy stalled with the advent of the 1970s economic crisis. How did this crisis come about and what were its consequences regarding state-led social reproduction?

THE LONG CRISIS

According to Giovanni Arrighi, great historian of capitalist crisis, the main sequences of global capitalism follow a similar pattern of growth and decay. Beginning with a period of capitalist expansion 'of the entire world economy' (1994:219–20), carried by manufacture and industrial capital, the markets gradually become saturated, spurring the expansion of finance capital to compensate for the slowdown in production through the increased trading and circulation of goods. Historically, the accumulation of finance capital has so far always spurred a new cycle of investment into production, thereby resetting and restarting the cycle again from the beginning in a different geographic centre. Applied to the United States, after the expansion of production through the war economies and the consumer boom of the mid twentieth century, we are today in a cycle of trade and circulation, indexed by the take-off of the FIRE (finance, insurance and real estate) sectors since the 1970s. However, economists have started to doubt that the productive economy can thereby be rekindled, and globally diminishing profit rates underwrite this trend. Contrary to the way the economy recovered from depression in the 1930s, the talk is thus of a qualitatively new and potentially terminal crisis.

Despite differences in the causal chains summoned to explain the contemporary crisis, economists agree that the early 1970s, specifically the year 1973, is the moment when the boom that characterised the period after WWII suddenly comes to an end. In the words of political theorist Joshua Clover:

> The year 1973 sees the first in a series of oil shocks, the formal withdrawal of the US from its Southeast Asian adventure, and the final collapse of the Bretton Woods monetary system setting the stage for increasing trade and current account imbalances; concomitant with these is a global downturn of markets. (2016b:130–31)

Clover's diagnosis, as well as his historical periodisation are based on Robert Brenner's influential account of the 'long downturn'. For Brenner, the 1970s come to stand for a profound crisis in US manufacture, in which Japanese and West German competitors challenge American hegemony by boosting production and driving down prices. Unable to reduce their productive capacity, American companies struggled to compete for market share, leading to 'overcapacity and overproduction in manufacturing on an international scale' (Brenner, 2006:38). How has capitalism attempted to solve this crisis? In line with Arrighi's argument that the credit system was called on to absorb the losses in manufacture, for political economist David McNally (2009), the favoured tool in the capitalist attempt to resolve the crisis in overproduction was financialisation, or the growth of financial tools and instruments, sold as bets on future gains.

The 1971 delinking of the dollar from the gold standard opened the door to a diverse array of financial products such as derivatives or credit default swaps that all speculate on anticipated future profits. While, as McNally highlights, the neoliberal turn of the 1980s produced a temporary recovery of profit margins (2011:26),[21] the net result of financialisation is an increasingly volatile economic environment, whose explosiveness was dramatically experienced in the 2008 credit bubble, which brought an end to capitalism's latest renewal. For McNally, the financial fix performed a shift from productive industries, based on labour, to increasingly 'fictitious capitals', based on banking, that culminated in factory closures, mass worker redundancies and layoffs across the globe.

Thus, it was workers who paid the price of this large-scale economic restructuring. This happened primarily through the mass unemployment that has befallen Western societies since the beginning of deindustrialisation in the late 1960s. Since 'fictitious capitals' need very little labour to function, the price of labour has been devalued at the same time as what Marx called the reserve army of labour, a growing surplus of workers that can be drafted in and out of employment at will has taken unprecedented dimensions.[22] This is what economist Loren Goldner captures when he speaks of a situation of generalised 'non-reproduction' (2007:66), meaning a depreciation of labour power, so intense that no new reproductive institutions (schools, hospitals, relief infrastructures) are built to benefit current and future workers..

Goldner concludes that we have entered a period of capitalist 'self-cannibalisation' (ibid.), since the investment into fictitious capital enables an enormous divestment of the means of basic social reproduction, resulting in mass unemployment, the concomitant increase in private debt, the privatisation of education and health care and a decaying public infrastructure. The flipside of finance capital's fantastic speculative power is thus a situation of social non-reproduction and the exploitation of entire populations, deemed superfluous and excluded from waged work. While capitalism has historically always been driven by crises, for Clover, 'the current period is distinguished from similar passages in previous cycles to the extent that recoveries of the sort seen previously remain from our vantage point invisible' (2016b:130).

The 1970s crisis put a definitive end to the early twentieth century dream of a peaceful co-development between capital and workers. At first, blue collar industrial work was scaled back, as factories in the industrial centres of Detroit or Newark closed down. While the white-collar FIRE sector and the service industry kept growing for a limited period of time, this shift drastically lessened workers' power as traditional models of unionisation and collective decision-making proved difficult to enact.[23] Beginning in the 1980s, white-collar employment also began to definitively slow down. This gradually pitted colleague against colleague and worker against worker in the battle for evermore scarce jobs.

As we have seen, the reaction of the US government to the decline in productive power has been a resolute scaling back of social spending in all areas of public life from education to disaster relief, creating a situation of 'contracted social reproduction' (Goldner, 2013: para. 2), in which diverse forms of reproductive labour increasingly have to be performed by communities themselves. We are thus faced with a bad dialectic between the spheres of the state and civil society, in which the state increasingly retreats from social reproduction, while including members of civil society in the administration of these services. At the same time, an increasing percentage of that very same civil society is today excluded from the elementary possibility of reproducing themselves through the wage, leading to a drastic rise in surplus populations. While a percentage of this surplus can be put to work as community organisers in the provision of a variety of volunteer-run services, thereby approximating capital's dream of a self-reproducing workforce,[24] a large percentage of them remains disenfranchised.

We can see that the form that the crisis takes in times of austerity is a renewed pressure on the domain of social reproduction, including welfare services, education, health care and disaster relief. The necessity of a social reproduction approach to disasters arises directly out of the reality of a long crisis in capital accumulation that started in the 1970s and shows no signs of abating. The current moment presents us with a new and unprecedented pressure on a growing number of workers, while at the same time shifting the political arena from productive waged work (the characteristic domain of the nineteenth century workers' movement) to the unwaged reproductive activities that have been side-lined by the labour movement. Hence the urgency and necessity to study those historical movements that have widened our political vocabulary by placing the *reproductive* activities of education, medical care and childcare at the head of the political agenda next to the *productive* work, validated by capitalism. The next chapter will examine one of the most paradigmatic of these movements and their attempt to self-organise social reproduction at the cusp of austerity, within and against the state.

5

1970: The Black Panthers' Quest for Dual Power

This administration here and now declares unconditional war on poverty.

— Lyndon B. Johnson

DISASTER, CRISIS AND SELF-ORGANISATION

Let us return then to the late 1960s and examine the beginning of the great economic crisis that brought to an end decades of capitalist expansion in the West. The mid-1960s represented a watershed in the administration of social reproduction in America. While, following desegregation, the federal state further extended its welfare profile to formerly marginalised communities, militant social movements began providing their own model of community-led social reproduction in response to the state's failure to live up to its promises of full employment and prosperity. This chapter examines one of the twentieth century's most successful attempts to self-organise social reproduction in conditions of structural disaster; the Black Panther Party for Self-Defense. Initially campaigning around issues of police violence, the organisation extended its reach by 1969 to encompass reproductive services such as a free breakfast for children programme and free health clinics.

Honing in on the relationship between state-led and community-led social reproduction, the chapter situates the Black Panther Party's transition from self-defence to self-organised social reproduction in the context of President Lyndon B. Johnson's Great Society welfare programmes. Contrasting the Panthers' self-organised community services with the state's federal policies of poverty and crime reduction, I argue that the Black Panther Party developed its' survival programs in direct response to the state, increasingly occupying the government's prerogatives in an attempt to rival the federal service provision in a game of dual power. I then argue that the Black Panthers' revolutionary bid to overthrow the state remained plagued by a significant contradiction, in that the party at the same time demanded better welfare services from that very same state. In conclusion, I point to the limits of self-organised social reproduction initiatives in an era when the state is expanding its welfare profile.

THE BLACK PANTHERS AND THE EMERGENCY

We, the people, are threatened with genocide because racism and fascism are rampant in this country [. . .] And the ruling circle in North America is responsible. (Newton, Hilliard et al., 2002:160)

With this, Huey P. Newton, the founder of the Black Panther Party for Self-Defense began his speech at Boston College on 18 November 1970. In that year, membership in the Black Panther Party peaked with thousands of enrolled members and established offices in over 68 cities across the US. Speaking to a numerous crowd, Newton laid out the Panthers' view that African Americans were threatened with extermination inside the United States of America. According to Newton, black Americans were systematically oppressed inside a white supremacist society that had only seemingly broken with slavery. Foreshadowing an argument that has recently gained traction in black studies, Newton argued that the abolition of slavery was not followed by freedom, as officially proclaimed, but merely transcribed the non-subjectivity of the slave into the limited subjecthood of the criminal, the ghetto dweller and the pauper.[25] Holding 'the ruling circle in North America' responsible, Newton indicts the US government for their fundamental disregard of black lives. In *The Correct Handling of a Revolution*, written in 1967, Newton specified that the founding of the party was to counter this existential threat: 'The main function of the party is to awaken the people and teach them the strategic method of resisting a power structure which is prepared not only to combat with massive brutality the people's resistance but to annihilate totally the Black population' (2002:143).

Newton's large audience shows how, what began as a small grassroots organisation, had by 1970 become a nationwide enterprise with considerable public appeal. While the Civil Rights Movement had through peaceful protest abolished the de jure segregation in the American South, de facto segregation remained operative in the north and west with permanent racial discrimination by housing associations, banks, employers and trade unions (Bloom and Martin 2013). According to the historian Donna Murch, Black Panther membership consisted of the sons and daughters of blacks from the South 'whose families travelled north and west to escape the southern racial regime, only to be confronted with new forms of segregation and repression' (2010:6). Contrary to the Civil Rights Movement that had demanded formal citizen rights for America's black population, the Panthers sought to fight the socio-economic marginalisation of blacks that persisted despite formal equality.

The philosopher Brady Thomas Heiner summarises the Black Panthers' perceived threats to their existence as, firstly, the view that black people constitute an internally colonised community within the US and are thus in a situation comparable to other anti-colonial struggles; secondly, that the US constitution, its laws and police work as functional agents in the oppression of blacks; thirdly, that within the context of this intranational colonisation, black self-defence was synonymous with anti-colonial war and, fourthly, that the American prison system played a pivotal role in the criminalisation of black people (2007:322). Beyond the legal equality, granted after desegregation, the Panthers thus diagnosed a structural violence at the heart of American civil society that was set to maintain the normative inferiority of blacks. Heiner explains how Newton's first theoretical move lay in unmasking the proclaimed peace in 1960s America, that he recast as a struggle over life and death:

> Beneath the law and order of the American government, beneath the ostensible peace of the American civil society, a racially fashioned war is being continuously and permanently waged against the black community. The type of peace that American governmental and civil institutions officially prescribe, according to this argument, is not genuinely pacific at all but rather is itself a form of coded warfare. (2007:322)

This radicalism was an expression of the black community's widespread disappointment with the consequences of American desegregation. After making illustrious promises to the Civil Rights Movement in the 1964 Civil Rights Act that outlawed racial discrimination and segregation, the American state was quickly falling short on its word. Rather than taking on the plight of the black population and ensuring its thriving in a postracial America, black families suffered the consequences of persistent poverty and unemployment. While the wartime weapons industries and the post-war industrial boom had provided jobs for tens of thousands of blacks, who emigrated north and west from the south, deindustrialisation started taking hold as early as 1960, plunging the recently migrated families into economic crisis. As the historian Robyn Spencer writes:

> Postwar demobilization displaced working-class blacks from the toehold they had been able to gain in shipbuilding and other defense industries. Manufacturing jobs disappeared as trucks replaced ships and trains as the major commercial freight carriers. Some African Americans were able to find work on railroads and docks, in local canneries, government installations, and, to a lesser extent, in domestic service. However, overall economic depression, high unemployment, underemployment, and low wages were the economic fate of many blacks in this period. (2016:8)

RIOTS PRODUCE REFORM

In the summer of 1964, this widespread poverty, alongside persistent racist harassment by a chiefly white police force, sparked the Harlem Riots. In response to the killing of a 15-year-old black teenager by a white policeman, rioting and looting broke out in the New York districts of Harlem and Bedford-Stuyvesant, with angry protesters demanding the indictment of the shooter. The riots that counted an estimated 4000 participants lasted six days, left one rioter dead, 118 protesters badly injured by police and 465 arrested (Shapiro and Sullivan 1964:18). The American government, under Lyndon B. Johnson's control since the assassination of John F. Kennedy, was deeply unsettled by the civil unrest and started to view the black community's poverty with increasing unease. According to Democrat policymakers, the riots showed that persistent poverty was dangerous for the national peace. The historian Elizabeth Hinton specifies that 'Johnson and allied policy makers understood urban citizen's decision to respond to their condition with violence' (2015:102–3). Consequently, and following the policymakers' logic, alleviating urban blacks' poverty would lead to diminished aggression and ultimately to increased civic peace.

Breaking with the classical liberal credo against income redistribution, President Johnson understood that the crisis-ridden economy by itself could not provide enough jobs to permanently ease black poverty. Terrified by the alleged dangers of a black lumpenproletariat, increasingly excluded from industrial labour, Johnson used his presidential powers and launched the nation's largest welfare initiative since the New Deal. Known as the Great Society programmes, the 1-billion-dollar welfare package began with Project Uplift, which responded directly to the Harlem Riots by creating hundreds of summer jobs for urban youth in New York, designed to keep teenagers busy and give them the skills to propel them into the workplace (Pinkney and Woock 1970:82). On the national level, the US government inaugurated the Department of Housing and Urban Development (HUD) in 1965, charged with building 600,000 new low-income homes, and launched Medicare and Medicaid, which offered health care services to poor communities. In addition, its Food Stamp Act drastically increased poor families' budgets for food, as well as offering free breakfast in schools.

However, while Johnson's policymakers accepted that the black community's propensity to civil unrest was rooted in poverty, they viewed the causes for poverty as originating in the behavioural specificities of black communities, rather than in the dynamics of capitalist crisis. Any policy that extended benefits to poor urban blacks was thus accompanied by wide-ranging crime control reforms that increased the policing of the new welfare recipients to keep offenses in check. If the Johnson administration's Great Society programme offered metaphorical carrots to poor African Americans, it therefore also disposed of a very real stick. Elizabeth Hinton describes how Johnson's war on poverty ran side by side a zealous war on crime:

> Johnson and many other liberals recognized poverty as the root cause of crime, but following Daniel Moynihan's hugely influential 1965 report, 'The Negro Family,' they also viewed community behavior and not structural exclusion as the cause of that poverty. To the policy makers reshaping American law enforcement, crime was an innate problem of black urban America, and—like a Soviet nuclear strike— something that might be targeted before it began if policy makers and foot soldiers possessed the proper tools. (2015:103)

Indeed, from their very inception, Johnson's Great Society programmes closely tied welfare provision to law enforcement through the Law Enforcement Assistance Act, passed together with Johnson's welfare package in 1965, which fundamentally reformed policing in the US. While the black community therefore immediately reaped the benefits of Johnson's welfare reform, it with the same immediacy suffered from increasingly draconian police measures.

The Law Enforcement Assistance Act crucially made law enforcement and social service provision work hand in hand, obliging welfare providers to work closely with local and federal police. Through the Act, social service agencies were obliged to report suspected delinquents to the police, as well as made to gather data on residents to create exhaustive criminal profiles, based on anticipated crime. As modern data gathering technologies improved, the police and welfare agencies began to use the same databases to administer benefits *and* maintain control of possible delinquents. As Elizabeth Hinton writes:

> In time, the entire spectrum of domestic social programs actively participated in national law enforcement, thereby pushing the boundaries of the carceral state beyond penal institutions. By [. . .] 1968, the carceral state had already begun to metastasize into a vast network of social programs originally created to combat racial exclusion and inequality. (2015:101–2)

Alongside data-driven and anticipatory crime control, the major effect of the Law Enforcement Assistance Act was the militarisation of urban policing itself. Breaking with the historical independence of state police departments, the Act subsumed local police activity under direct federal authority. Under its aegis, thousands of new officers were drafted into police departments to patrol black neighbourhoods. Furthermore, the federal government enabled supplementary funds to substantially enhance local police equipment with surveillance and weapons technologies, such as helicopters and tanks that had been tried and tested in the Vietnam War. According to Johnson's policymakers, the necessity for such muscular policing arose directly from the threat of urban race riots, for which Harlem had set a precedent. As President Johnson proclaimed that 'we are today fighting a war in our own boundaries' (cited in Hinton, 2015:103), the new anti-riot measures encouraged police to view their relation to the black community as akin to warfare. Elizabeth Hinton confirms that:

> Under the new legislation, the federal government financially encouraged states to acquire surplus M-1 military carbines, army tanks, bulletproof vests, and walkie-talkies for local police by covering up

to 90 percent of the costs of riot-prevention programs, which were defined broadly. And despite the reputation of the [. . .] antiriot squads for harassing black activists and imposing stop-and-frisk searches on young residents, Congress promoted such units by authorizing [. . .] to cover 75 percent of their cost. (ibid.)

However, against the legislators' predictions, the new poverty and crime control programmes did not ease tensions between the state and the black community. Instead, black activists responded belligerently to the increased policing of their neighbourhoods, as standoffs between residents and the police became more frequent. Rather than bringing peace and prosperity, the Great Society era saw the worst outbreaks of violence the US had experienced since the Civil War, with riots flaring up in Watts in 1965, then in Newark and Detroit in 1967 and in 125 different cities following the 1968 assassination of Martin Luther King. In each of these incidents, black protesters confronted an ever more militarised police force. Consequently, each incident saw an ever-higher number of black civilian casualties.

SELF-DEFENCE

These violent background conditions help us understand the circumstances that led to the founding of the Black Panther Party in 1966, as well as the Panthers' advocacy of self-defence as a core political strategy. Crucially, the party's first activity consisted in creating armed groups that patrolled the police with guns and law book in hand to prevent harassment. These actions were perfectly legal, since the Panthers exploited a loophole in California State Law that allowed civilians to carry weapons, if openly displayed. Paying like with like, the Black Panthers began policing the police, in response to the state's enhanced law enforcement patrols. As Robyn Spencer describes:

[The Panthers] began to monitor the actions of the Oakland Police Department, poised to intervene with tape recorders, cameras, law books, and legally carried firearms. Typically, Newton and Seale would observe police as they arrested people to make sure the officers were not breaking laws or using excessive force [. . .] The sight of two young black men, carrying guns, loudly asserting their right to bear arms and warning the police not to be the aggressors repeatedly drew crowds. (2016:40)

Countering the state's violence with self-defence was a key tactic in the early days of the Black Panthers. Aiming to recruit fresh party members through their actions, the Panthers politicised their everyday life as a fight over life and death. In response to the failure of the US state to deliver on the promises of the Civil Rights Act, the Panthers in turn radically withdrew their responsibility to hold civic peace. The notorious documentation of Panther members patrolling the streets of Oakland with shotguns poised, pictures of Newton posing on an African throne, spear and rifle in hand as tokens of Black Nationalism and the seizure of Attica prison in New York, where imprisoned Panthers held 42 prison guards hostage show how the Panthers paid the state back in kind by staging their own violent spectacle in response to the increasing state violence. Countering President Johnson's war on crime, the Panthers began to spectacularly wage war on the police. Brady Thomas Heiner comments on the equation of politics and war that was at the heart of early Black Panther discourse: 'It is precisely on account of this perceived failure of American sovereignty to guarantee and protect black people's very right to live – moreover, on account of its persistent and explicit attack on that right – that the BPP conceived of politics and war as functionally inseparable'. (2007:325)

This radicalism found admirers in European intellectuals from Michel Foucault to Gilles Deleuze, who had started theorising politics on the basis of war after the events of May '68 in Paris.[26] Jean Genet, who visited Newton in California defended the Panther leaders' spectacular display of violence: 'Wherever they went the Americans were the masters, so the Panthers should do their best to terrorize the masters by the only means available to them. Spectacle. And the spectacle would work because it was the product of despair [. . .] Did they have any choice?' (2003:99)

The politics of armed spectacle enjoyed an ambivalent success during the early days of the Black Panthers. While on the one hand, it swelled the ranks of the party by attracting many disenfranchised blacks, frustrated with California's dwindling economic opportunities and persistent racism, it ran the risk of reducing the Black Panthers' variegated political tactics to the image of the gun. As Robyn Spencer writes:

> Emphasizing self-defense in the bpp's early actions would heighten the party's visibility, attract their first members, and garner national attention. However, it also created publicity that Newton and Seale

were unable to define or control as they gained notoriety not for their political analyses but for their armed stance. (2016:37)

In his chronicle of the Black Panther Party, the activist and party co-founder Bobby Seale recounts how many new Panther members joined the party in order to revel in its armed militancy. He tells the story of the new party member Tarika Lewis, whose second question upon meeting Seale was if she too could have a gun: 'Some brothers [and sisters] would come into the Party, and see us with guns, and they related only to the gun' (cited in Spencer, 2016:49), Seale complained. Indeed, Panther membership rose exponentially after every outburst of spectacular violence. The death of the Panther treasurer and first recruit Bobby Hutton, aged 18, at the hands of the police, and the conviction of Huey Newton for the murder of a policeman (Newton was later acquitted and released from prison) spurred mass protest against the police and led to new Panther chapters opening all across the country.

In more ways than one, armed self-defence was a double-edged sword for the Black Panthers, as their open embrace of violence also meant that membership made its holders susceptible to surveillance by the FBI's counter-intelligence operations of defamation and criminalisation (COINTELPRO) that sought to outlaw Panther activities. As Robyn Spencer writes: 'Armed self-defence exposed the raw nerve of state repression as Oakland's local police forces responded to the Panthers' armed initiatives with surveillance and harassment and conservative politicians sought to sew shut the loophole that made the Panthers' weapons legal' (2016:38).

Armed escalation was a Janus-faced affair for the Panthers; both increasing membership, as well as putting more and more party members on the line of police violence. As a consequence, the question of armed self-defence became a divisive one within the party, and after Newton's release from jail, the Panthers gradually abandoned armed escalation in exchange for community services.

SELF-ORGANISATION

Newton's gradual distancing from the spectacular violence he had endorsed in the 1960's and his turn towards a politics of welfare provision can be traced most clearly in his dispute with the Panthers' Minister of Information Eldridge Cleaver. While Cleaver wanted to push the Party into full-blown armed warfare, Newton opposed this position. Abandoning his provocations in favour of a more attenuated politics, he argued from 1970 onwards that armed resistance was bound to be overpowered by the military superiority of the American police and that, rather than all-out war, the Panthers should adopt a politics of restrained resistance. In an article from 1967, he claimed:

> The Black masses are handling the resistance incorrectly. When the brothers in East Oakland [. . .] amassed the people in the streets, threw bricks and Molotov cocktails to destroy property and create disruption, they were herded into a small area by the gestapo police and immediately contained by the brutal violence of the oppressor's storm troops. Although this manner of resistance is sporadic, short-lived, and costly, it has been transmitted across the country to all the ghettos of the Black nation. (2002:142)

Instead of paramilitary activities, the BPP now began to invest strongly into their so-called Survival Programs, a range of over 24 community service programmes that the party ran free of charge to benefit the black population. The programmes included a breakfast-for-schools initiative, in which breakfast was served to children before the start of the school day; health and dental clinics, where medical services were provided, a sickle-cell anaemia screening program; a buses to prisons service that transported families to and from prison to visit their relatives; a clothing program and various cultural activities, such as a model school, music, poetry and Black History classes. In a televised interview with the talk show host William Buckley, Newton explained this shift from an emphasis on armed escalation to an investment in community services:

> We realized that it wasn't the principle of revolution or the armed principle of our Party, to take the gun and make the gun the only thing that could fight a revolution. So, it was a strategy that was mistaken [. . .] The media enjoyed the sensationalism of the gun. In many ways, we set ourselves up for the murder we received [. . .] We realized that we had to treat the issues that the people were most concerned about. (2002:276)

While Newton still framed the need for the social programmes as stemming from the threat of genocide and the necessity for black survival, he simultaneously highlighted a quality in survival that seems to escape the struggle over life and death through the affective categories of self-respect, dignity and enthusiasm:

> A Ten-Point Program is not revolutionary in itself, nor is it reformist. It is a survival program. We, the people, are threatened with genocide because racism and fascism are rampant in this country and throughout the world. And the ruling circle in North America is responsible. We intend to change all of that, and in order to change it, there must be a total transformation. But until we can achieve that total transformation, we must exist. In order to exist, we must survive; therefore, we need a survival kit [. . .] It is necessary for our children to grow up healthy with functional and creative minds [. . .] Where there is courage, where there is self-respect and dignity, there is a possibility that we can change the conditions and win. This is called *revolutionary enthusiasm*. (2002:160–1)

The Survival Programs were destined to elevate the morale of their beneficiaries and make them receptive to the affect of revolution. More importantly, they had a strong temporal function, stretching the passive time pending death into the active time of survival, a time of holding out and holding on until the right time for revolution had come. They thereby mark Newton's sustained engagement with what one might call a revolutionary philosophy of time. In the article *On the Defection of Eldridge Cleaver*, Newton highlighted that a dispute around time was at the core of his disagreement with Cleaver. While Cleaver 'ordered everyone into the streets tomorrow' (2002:207), Newton knew that 'a spontaneous revolution is a fantasy' (ibid.). Rather than provoking a revolutionary conflict in the here-and-now, the BPP's inflection around 1970 inaugurated a sustained investment into resistance and survival. Differentiating between resistance and revolution, the philosopher Howard Caygill comments on the temporal difference between a revolutionary acceleration of time and the prolonged effort to extend the capacity to resist: 'A capacity is precisely a prolongation in time – thus, the struggle for resistance occupies an extended time horizon, unlike the revolutionary bid for power which thrives on the acceleration of time' (2013:10).

The Panthers' welfare programmes exemplify this marked shift from a politics of escalation to a sustained politics of survival. Investing into the physical wellbeing of the people, as well as into their cultural education, they opened a sheltered space where the black community could exist outside the immediate pressures of direct confrontation and struggle. Their Survival Programs carved out a niche of life that for a time withstood the FBI's counter-intelligence operations of defamation and criminalisation. During this time, Newton carefully guarded against advocating the revolution *now*, while promoting the belief in the longevity and eventual triumph of the movement.

If armed escalation had worked well in the short term to mobilise the black community around the issue of police violence, the self-organisation of social reproduction worked even better. The black community enthusiastically welcomed the Panthers' change from armed escalation to community service, as it offered many people a point of identification beyond the gun and standoffs with the police. For the first time, the Panthers drew support from a wide segment of their constituency, from black shop owners to farmers and the black middle class. Robyn Spencer cites the approving testimonies of women, active in the Breakfast for Schools programme:

> [Ruth] Beckford recalled that there was a lot of community support. A black dairy owner delivered milk every morning and a local bakery donated donuts [. . .] They felt that this was a very positive program for the Panthers. Where others might have been afraid of any association with the Panthers 'cause they thought that they were violent, ... this program was their strongest point and was able to rally people from all sections of the community [. . .] The community response was great. People saw that we were not just out here being wild and carrying guns: we were really trying to make a difference. And that was the way I felt we were accepted into the community. (2016:85)

RIVALLING THE STATE

While it was new and revolutionary for a social movement to enter the realm of social reproduction, it is striking that in both their police patrols, as well as in their community services, the Panthers essentially mirrored practices that had been established by Johnson's Great Society programmes two years prior to the founding of the party. The armed patrolling of the police emulated the war on crime's new law enforcement patrols, while reversing its roles. The breakfast-for-schools programme had been established by the Johnson administration in 1965, four years before the Panthers began feeding children before the school day. Even their sickle cell anaemia screening echoed Johnson's Medicaid and Medicare programmes. How can we make sense of the competition between the state and the Black Panther Party on the terrain of social reproduction? In recent political theory, the Panthers' strategy of emulating prerogatives of the state to create their own autonomous service network has gained renewed scholarly appraisal under the heading of dual power.

Dual power theorists argue that the Black Panthers' social programmes constituted a revolutionary attempt to organise an alternative network of welfare provision that rivalled the state in efficiency and delivery, effectively creating a second power hub, parallel to, and separate from the state. In his recent reflections on dual power, political theorist Fredric Jameson argues that at the extreme end of crisis, there is always the possibility of dual power to emerge. In Jameson's account, dual power develops when a social organisation occupies terrains that are officially prerogatives of the state, such as health care, public transportation or garbage collection, and begins to rival the state in providing these services. Dual power is intimately tied to crisis, since it is during crisis that it becomes markedly clear that the state often fails to provide these basic duties. In Jameson's words:

> I would most notably single out the way organizations like the Black Panthers yesterday or Hamas today function to provide daily services – food kitchens, garbage collection, health care, water inspection, and the like – in areas neglected by some official central government [. . .] In such situations, power moves to the networks to which people turn for practical help and leadership on a daily basis: in effect, they become an alternate government, without officially challenging the ostensibly legal structure. (2016:4)

Jameson's engagement with dual power, published alongside a selection of critical commentaries, consciously responds to a current impasse in the progressive imagination. Jameson's starting point is that today, both a revolutionary overthrow of the state and state reforms towards a more humane capitalism have dramatically failed: 'Social democracy is in our time irretrievably bankrupt, and communism seems dead' (2016:3). In the face of the exhaustion of the twentieth century's rich political spectrum, the historical anomaly of dual power gains a new relevance for Jameson and his commentators. Dual Power has its origin in the peculiar situation in Russia between the implosion of tsarism and the October Revolution, when the different factions of soviets, workers' and soldiers' councils all vied for power. The political philosopher Alberto Toscano comments on Lenin's incisive observations of the extraordinary phenomenon of dual power in Russia:

> Lenin stresses the unprecedented emergence of a wild anomaly in the panorama of political forms: dual power. As he remarks in Pravda, 'alongside the Provisional Government, the government of the bourgeoisie, another government has arisen, so far weak and incipient, but undoubtedly a government that actually exists and is growing'. (2016:217–18)

While Jameson indulges in a utopian thought experiment on the potential of locating dual power in the armed forces, Alberto Toscano provides more concrete, actually existing examples of dual power structures that may autonomously organise social reproduction in face of persistent governmental neglect. Following on from the young Soviet Union, Toscano lists the establishment of 'self-valorising' 'liberated zones' in 1960s Italy (2016:224), 'the incomplete experiences of dual power in Bolivia and Chile in the early seventies' (ibid.:221), the breakfast and health service programmes of the Black Panther Party, as well as the provision of clean drinking water by the Lebanese Hezbollah as organised attempts that 'thrived on the systematic use of the duality power' (ibid.:226).

According to Toscano, what these initiatives have in common is their attention to the essential processes of social reproduction, understood as the care and maintenance of the welfare of the population. This biopolitical component gains an increasingly acute dimension in times when the state is gradually but decisively withdrawing from providing these reproductive services:

> Within this volatile geometry of forces, the 'biopolitical' element provides much of the substance of dual power [. . .] We could even say that the 'biopolitical supplement' to the neoliberal evacuation of services and solidarity is inextricable and primary vis-à-vis any mere military strategy [. . .] We could call [this] a kind of dual biopower— which is to say the collective attempt to appropriate politically

aspects of social reproduction that state and capital have abandoned or rendered unbearably exclusionary, from housing to medicine. (ibid.:228)

Concretely, what provides the trigger, as well as the battlefield for dual power are thus the biological cycles of health, nutrition and bodily welfare. For Toscano, this constitutes a decisive shift in the terrain of struggles away from production and towards reproduction, which he, much like Howard Caygill in his reflections on resistance, discusses as a shift in the temporality of political struggle. Dual power challenges us to think the multiple and incommensurable temporalities of entangled social and economic forms that might be at odds with the understanding of capitalist development as a linear, progressive process. In another essay, Toscano turns to the philosopher Étienne Balibar and the latter's theory of the lag (*décalage*) in order to make sense of the practices of dual power and group their diverse historical expressions under a unified conceptual heading. For Toscano, rather than the politics of immediacy, expressed in the revolt, the riot or similar outburst of social negation, at stake in dual power is the delineation of a concept of transition 'conceived of as times of unevenness and conflict' (2014:765), in which an autonomous support structure can effectively arise and take hold. Consequently, dual power works as an alternative third term to our tired 'reform-revolution and revolt-revolution dichotomies' (ibid.:762).

For Toscano, following Balibar, the distinction between cycles of production and reproduction constitutes the primary arena for dual power. While cycles of production, from agriculture to industry and beyond, may be historicised in a relatively linear way, drawing on technological innovation or developments in labour organisation, social reproduction, as the types of work that reconstitute labour power and ensure the continuation of the social structure forms the overlooked social substrate that enables these varying productive relations and that moves slower than production. Reproduction is understood by Toscano to cut 'across continuity and discontinuity' (ibid.:766), enabling what he calls a '*décalage* or 'non-correspondence' between different levels or components of the social formation' (ibid.:768). This non-correspondence gives social reproduction its autonomy. It is this lag that dual power organisations exploit in their attempts to autonomously manage social reproduction.

Thinkers of dual power in the wake of Jameson agree that dual power provides 'ways of rooting the need to undo capitalist relations in the real, if partial, experience of attempts to limit its powers' (Toscano, 2016:229). However, despite the Panthers' success at organising support for their community, as a revolutionary strategy, their survival programmes failed. This certainly had a lot to do with the aggressive subversion of the Panthers by the state and the FBI. But I argue that it is just as much related to the specific management of American social reproduction in the 1960s, specifically, the expansion of the US welfare state, which limited the reach of self-organised social reproduction as a revolutionary strategy. Let us conclude by elucidating some of these historical reasons.

THE RUSES OF STATE-LED SOCIAL REPRODUCTION

First, let us point out that theorists of dual power, from Lenin to Jameson do not classically write at a time of welfare state expansion. For Lenin, writing at the turn of the twentieth century, the welfare state would not emerge for another 30 years. For Jameson on the other hand, the welfare state had come and gone for around 30 years. As a revolutionary theory and practice, dual power was elaborated at a time of minimal state-led social reproduction, in which the burden of reproductive labour was almost exclusively shouldered by civil society. Indeed, most of the case studies that dual power theorists use to illustrate the phenomenon, such as the Mexican Zapatistas or the Lebanese Hezbollah, operate in a zone of utter welfare state retrenchment, in which social movements, in Alberto Toscano's words, seek 'to gain relative hegemony over a population side-lined by a fragmented, unequal and threadbare state' (2006:155).

When faced with an absent state, adopting the strategy of dual power has a strong practical, as well as performative function. In such moments, filling the glaring gaps in the state service provision through community organising can respond to real material needs, as well as leverage polit-ical power by mobilising community support. By taking over former terrains of the state, social movements can spectacularly emphasise gov-ernmental neglect by flashing up the state's refusal to deliver essential reproductive services. Commenting on the breakfast-for-schools pro-gramme, Robyn Spencer highlights how the Panthers had exactly this in mind. Their double-strategy lay in firstly, exposing the state's unwilling-ness to deliver this essential service, and secondly, in demonstrating the superiority of their own self-organised social welfare: 'Seale argued that the program could highlight the government's failure to provide such a crucial social service, as well as add another dimension to their public image and potentially broaden their base of support' (2016:85).

What, however, becomes of dual power at a time when the state is increasingly reaching out to communities in need? In those times, state-led social reproduction takes away some of the thrust of self-organised welfare, since the terrain of social reproduction is not immediately visible as a terrain of class struggle. Rather, in a situation like this, communities come to depend on the state, just as they depend on wage labour. Indeed, despite their resolutely anti-state stance, the Black Panthers displayed a thorny adherence to both the state and to capitalism in their self-organisation of social reproduction. Not only did their self-defense and survival programmes structurally copy the Johnson administration's anti-poverty and anti-crime policies. In their very administration, they actually utilised state resources to determine their community's welfare needs, making the difference between worker's inquiry and governmental inquiry increasingly slim.[27] The historians Salar Mohandesi and Emma Teitelman have outlined how the Panthers repurposed the state's existing welfare infrastructure:

> It is well known that Bobby Seale and Huey Newton [. . .] developed their party's program at the North Oakland Neighborhood Anti-Poverty Center, where they used federal resources. [. . .] The party even used the government's lists of welfare recipients to perform inquiries into 'the desires of the community,' as Newton put it. (2017:59)

However, more than simply utilising the state's resources for their own means on the level of political practice, the Panthers also displayed a peculiar adherence to the state on the level of party theory. This attachment can be summarised in a simple performative contradiction: While the Panthers called on the black community to overthrow the United States government, their 10 Point Program at the same time demanded improved welfare services from that very same state.[28] Indeed, the very initiative to provide social services in lieu of the state, stemmed from the wounded desire that the state had not taken enough responsibility for the black community's plight. This sense of outrage and hurt is legible in every twist and turn of the 10 Point Program, in which, while calling on the black community to overthrow the federal government, the Panthers at the same time held: 'The federal government [. . .] responsible and obligated to give every person employment or a guaranteed income [. . .]

The government must provide free of charge for the people, health facilities [. . .] to guarantee our future survival' (1972:96).

This contradictory relationship to state-led social reproduction as something at once desired and contested characterises many civil-society-led social reproduction initiatives. As radical as the Black Panthers stance was vis-à-vis the state, the group at the same time displayed a strong desire that the state should be more receptive to their community's misery. The same ambiguity is present in the Black Panthers' relationship to the black business elite, whom they at once solicited for donations, and sought to abolish, along with the capitalist state.

From its inception, boycotting businesses believed to operate racist shop floor practices constituted a core tactic of the Black Panther Party. In 1971, the Panthers joined the California State Package Store and Tavern Owners Association (Cal-Pac)'s boycott of Oakland's Mayfair Supermarket, rumoured to practice discriminatory hiring policies. However, when in the wake of the alliance, Cal-Pac's director, the black businessman William Boyette, could only be moved to a measly one-off donation to the party's coffers, the Panthers quickly turned on him, and, citing the collusion of black capitalists with the white supremacist state, called for a state-wide boycott of Cal-Pac. Newton summarised the Panthers' stance as follows:

> We see very little difference between Blacks who make profits from the Black community and refuse to contribute to Black survival programs and the white profiteers, such as Mayfair...If they refuse to help the Black community they are parasites that must be forced out of business through economic boycott. Why should the Black community nourish a Black profiteer who has no concern for his brother. (cited in Spencer, 2016:127)

However, as donations by black capitalists proved too important for the party to completely relinquish, and since the party had no qualms about accepting donations from white capitalists, it was eventually forced to change its stance on the nature of black capitalism. Instead of viewing black capitalists as race traitors who were making profits on the back of their disenfranchised community, Newton soon sought a renewed dialogue with those black business leaders who freely gave to the Black Panthers. In a dialectical tour de force, Newton now claimed that by giving to black neighbourhoods, the black capitalist was actually engaged in an act of self-abolition that actively contributed to the destruction of capitalism by strengthening the capital-negating forces of the black community:

> There is no salvation in capitalism, but through this new approach the Black capitalist will contribute to his own negation by helping to build a strong political vehicle which is guided by revolutionary concepts and serves as a vanguard for the people . . . So we will heighten the contradiction between the Black community and corporate capitalism, while at the same time reducing the contradiction between the Black capitalist and the Black community. In this way Black capitalism will be transformed from a relationship of exploitation of the community to a relationship of service to the community, which will contribute to the survival of everyone. (cited in Spencer, 2016:124)

In their relation to the state and to capitalism, the Panthers thus adopted the contradictory, but highly dialectical strategy of 'within and against', using state and market resources with the aim of pushing their inherent contradictions to a point of collapse. Seeing themselves as the agents of the coming revolution, the Panthers believed that anything that strengthened them – be it services from the state or donations from capital – would ultimately lead to their dominance, and consequently, to the system's demise. Beyond dialectics, however, this dependence of civil-society-led social reproduction on the state in times of welfare state expansion points to a real limit of dual power as a revolutionary strategy. In reality, Johnson's Great Society programmes simply benefitted poor communities too much for their recipients to seriously challenge the government. As Mohandesi and Teitelman sum up:

> The expansion of social welfare programs had undeniable benefits for working-class men and women. Workers led healthier lives; enjoyed greater access to housing, education, and food; and could count on the state to compensate for lost income from old age, illness, disabilities, or unemployment. For many households in the United States, particularly those in poverty, federal assistance became central to everyday survival. (2017:59)

The radical improvement of working-class lives under the Great Society policies led a growing number of social movements to increasingly adopt the welfare state's tenets into its programmes. Often, this took the form of increased demands on the state. Thus, while the radical feminist collective Wages for Housework framed their struggle around domestic labour in the welfare state's vocabulary of fair payments and salaries, the Black Panthers remained torn between calls to abolish the state and capital and solicitations for governmental and business handouts. This dilemma could not be solved under the confines of the welfare state that sucked the energy out of dual power strategies of self-organisation. Indeed, the Johnson administration only further expanded its welfare portfolio during the 1960s. By 1970, it extended its Food Stamp programme to families above the poverty line, making the argument that the state was not doing its job increasingly difficult to uphold.

With the advent of the 1973 economic crisis however, the state soon changed course on the administration of social reproduction. Following a steep drop in its industrial profits, the country experienced a spike in inflation and a rise in unemployment. In response to what became known as stagflation, i.e. simultaneous economic stagnation and inflation, the US government ushered in austerity measures in the 1980s and 1990s to radically reduce the cost of state-led social reproduction, plunging the deindustrialised working class into a deep reproductive crisis. At the same time, new participatory policies incentivised community leaders to increasingly work together with local governments, rather than against them, dealing another blow to resistant forms of self-organisation. With no significant civil-society-led initiatives to fill the ensuing gap in social reproduction, the terrain of class struggle shifted in the 1980s and 1990s to the sphere that, for President Johnson's policymakers came hand in hand with the war on poverty; the war on crime.

6

1995: Poverty, Crime and the Heat

*If you look at the war on drugs from a purely economic point of view, the
role of the government is to protect the drug cartel. That's literally true.*
— Milton Friedman

CHICAGO IS MELTING

In mid-July 1995, an intense heat wave, carrying the second hottest
weather ever locally recorded, hit Chicago. Temperatures climbed to 106
degrees Fahrenheit (41 degrees Celsius) for several days and turned the
city into a giant cauldron. Warned of the heat by the media and local
politicians, Chicagoans braced themselves and developed coping mechanisms, ranging from the leisurely to the desperate. Kids shot water pistols
in the streets, while their parents sipped cool drinks in the shade. Residents took to the city beaches with as many as 90,000 people filling a
crammed downtown beach. Students slept with wet towels as blankets
to cool down in their sweltering halls of residence. As cars broke down
and trains detached from their moorings, the city traffic ground to a
halt. The Chicago Police began watering bridges to prevent the concrete
from locking, as the slabs expanded in the heat. Fire fighters hosed down
children stuck in school buses to stop them from fainting, as the city vac-
illated between frenzy and torpor. Observing the events at the height of
the summer, the sociologist and Chicago native Eric Klinenberg noted:
'Tuesday, July 12; sunny and still; temperature near 100; heat index 102;
the streets ablaze; the air sticky; almost thick enough to chew' (1999:246).

Things turned serious as temperatures kept rising throughout the
week, with no significant drop during night-time. Everyone who owned
air conditioning kept it running on full blast, leading to skyrocketing
electricity consumption that caused citywide power outages when the
electricity provider Commonwealth Edison proved unprepared for such
heat. With no air conditioning, apartments heated up quickly, gradually
making inside and outside indistinguishable. In a desperate search for

cooling, teenagers opened fire hydrants with sledgehammers to create makeshift water fountains, temporarily relieving whole neighbourhoods from the heat. Unfortunately for those who stayed inside, the manoeuvre caused the water pressure to drop, resulting in many apartments being cut off from running water for hours. This episode also entailed the first outbursts of violence, as police began shutting down hydrants and issuing a fine for everyone caught in the act of cooling. In a doomed attempt to keep the hydrants open, youth in the inner city 'showered nine water department trucks with gunfire, bricks or rocks and caused minor injuries to four workers.'[29]

With the power out, residents increasingly fell ill. Emergency responders sometimes took up to two hours to reach a citizen in need. Often they came too late. Chicagoans began dying by the dozen from heat stroke and from exhaustion. Over the days, the city morgues filled up with hundreds of dead residents piling up in front of the cooling chambers. In a bizarre act of philanthropy, a Chicago trucking company donated a fleet of 48 foot-long meat-packing trucks to provide a temporary storage place for the corpses (Klinenberg 1999:250).

Chicagoans not working in the medical sector were oblivious to the high death rate, but when temperatures dropped, the shocking facts of the disaster that claimed more lives than the Oklahoma City bombing (1995) and Hurricane Andrew (1992) combined became apparent. As Eric Klinenberg recapitulates:

By the end of the week [. . .] few could deny that the city had witnessed a disaster of historical proportion: medical examiners confirmed that over five-hundred Chicagoans had died directly from the heat, public health workers reported over seven-hundred deaths in excess of the weekly average, and hospitals registered thousands of visits for weather-related problems. (1999:240)

Attempting to protect Chicago's public image, politicians and the media played up the 'natural' components of the disaster. As the Democratic Mayor Richard Daley reasoned: 'Every day, people die of natural causes. You can't put everything as heat related [. . .] Then everybody in the summer that dies will die of the weather' (cited in Klinenberg 1999:273). Others were not content with this explanation. Arguing that the disproportionate death rate during the heat wave bore social rather than

natural causes, researchers from a variety of disciplines began investigating the matter.

DYING ALONE

Among the first to address the issue was the epidemiologist Jan Semenza,
who examined the health factors that influenced vulnerability during the
heat wave. Based on the mortality data gathered by the Cook County
Medical Examiner's Office that had registered the peak in heat-related
deaths, Semenza ran a large-scale statistical analysis to find out what
determined heat wave mortality. The epidemiologist found that the vast
majority of heat wave victims were elderly people. Additionally, Semenza
isolated the parameter of 'living alone' as a major risk factor. According
to the epidemiologist, elderly people who lived alone or rarely left their
house were twice as likely to perish during extended heat spells than
people who had regular social contact (Semenza 1996:86).

Building on this research in his monograph *Heat Wave*, Klinenberg
further attempted to unmask the social facts that lay hidden beneath the
official narrative of a tragic 'natural' disaster. His report put forward a
bold hypothesis: Rather than unnaturally hot weather, it was Chicago's
high crime rate that led to excessive senior citizen vulnerability during
the heat wave. The highest amount of heat wave deaths occurred among
seniors in neighbourhoods replete with violent crime. According to
Klinenberg, high crime led elderly residents to develop a 'bunker mentality' and board themselves up indoors, a strategy which proved fatal
during the heat.

Klinenberg's findings were in turn contested by the sociologist Mitchell
Duneier, who argued for poverty, rather than crime as a major vulnerability factor during the heat wave (Duneier 2004). Chiming in with disaster
scholars, suggesting a strong link between social class, ill health and
elevated disaster vulnerability (Lindsay 2003; Barusch 2011:347; Lowe,
Ebi and Forsberg 2013:7017), Duneier argued that income and its strong
correlation with health status were sufficient reasons to explain the high
death rate of senior citizens during the heat wave without recourse to
crime or social isolation as additional causal factors.

As much as senior citizen poverty and high youth crime may have
affected mortality during the heat wave, in this chapter, I argue that
sociological explanations of disaster vulnerability fall short in a significant way. Obsessed with isolating causal mortality factors, they are

unable to recognise the systemic conditions that make populations vulnerable; not only during a momentary calamity but in everyday life. Where disaster studies singles out isolated vulnerability factors, a social reproduction approach to disaster analyses what connects these factors in a specific mode of production and reproduction. Inverting disaster studies' question of how communities' everyday lives become ruptured, we should instead ask what these ruptures reveal about communities' everyday lives. In this perspective, disasters open up privileged vistas onto ongoing social crises, above and beyond momentary emergencies. Focussing only on individual vulnerability factors obfuscates disaster's *longue durée*, making its endemic nature disappear behind a spectacular smokescreen.

Marshalling such an approach, this chapter follows disaster scholars' singling out of youth crime and senior poverty as particular vulnerability factors and shows their interconnectedness in the unfolding economic crisis. From the standpoint of social reproduction, both high youth crime, as well as elevated senior poverty become legible as the differential effects of the mid-century restructuring of social reproduction towards austerity. While during the Chicago Heat Wave, this reproductive crisis became particularly visible, its damage had been decades in the making. Moreover, tying disaster vulnerability to economic crisis enables us to demand thoroughgoing political and economic change to diminish the effects of disaster in a longer-lasting way than the piecemeal policy changes, suggested by vulnerability scholars can.

How does Klinenberg arrive at his diagnosis of high crime as a major vulnerability factor during the heat wave? The sociologist builds on and initially confirms the epidemiologists Jan Semenza's findings. Accessing police reports, filed by the officers who retrieved heat wave victims from their homes, Klinenberg notes the frequent mention of victims that 'lived alone [or] were recluses' (2002:55), corroborating old age and social isolation as primary risk factors. However, Klinenberg goes on to criticise Semenza's study and suggests enhancing it in a substantial way. While the epidemiologist demonstrated a good grasp of at-risk groups, according to Klinenberg, he failed to provide an analysis of neighbourhood variation within vulnerable groups, thereby omitting relevant social causes for heat wave mortality. While it may be true that the elderly were 'generally' more vulnerable to heat than the young, Klinenberg argues this gives us a falsely homogenous image of heat wave vulnerability. Seeking to correct this oversight, he proposes a 'social-ecological analysis of urban health' (2002:81) that compares distinct neighbourhood properties to gain an insight into what Klinenberg calls 'place-based death' (ibid.:85).

DOWN IN LAWNDALE

In order to develop a 'critical neighbourhood analysis' of disaster vulnerability that is sensitive to place-specific variations, Klinenberg selects two adjacent neighbourhoods, the predominantly African American North Lawndale and the predominantly Latino South Lawndale as his investigative sites. Finding them almost identical in their proportions of seniors living alone and seniors living in poverty, they nevertheless display a stark contrast in heat wave mortality of 19 heat-related deaths (North Lawndale) to 3 heat-induced deaths (South Lawndale), apparently making them the ideal pair to distil hitherto unrecognised mortality factors.

Klinenberg firstly observes the architectural and infrastructural degradation of North Lawndale, which he compares to the burgeoning infrastructure of its southern sibling:

> It takes only a few minutes of observation in the two community areas [. . .] to see that the two Lawndales are [. . .] totally different worlds [. . .] The physical landscape of North Lawndale's largest thoroughfares and many of its residential streets is dominated by boarded or dilapidated buildings, rickety fast-food joints, closed stores with faded signs, and open lots where tall grass and weeds and broken glass, and illegally dumped refuse give testament to the area's decline. (2002 92)

The story of North Lawndale shares with many other Midwestern working class African American neighbourhoods after deindustrialisation. When the heavy industry companies Sears and Western Electric moved their headquarters in the 1960s, following the heavy rioting after the assassination of Martin Luther King, the formerly buoyant neighbourhood experienced a rapid growth in unemployment. Unable to find work locally, many residents were forced to move away. Together with the 'white flight' that began when black labourers migrated northward after the end of segregation, the new wave of black economic refugees decimated the population of North Lawndale, leaving 40% of the neighbourhood's land vacant by 1990 (Klinenberg 2002:98). Drawing on governmental statistics, Klinenberg concludes that the overwhelming cumulative effect of high unemployment, population decline, mass poverty and governmental neglect is the rise of urban crime. Citing data from the Chicago Police Department, Klinenberg argues that North Lawndale – despite having a crime rate below the most dangerous Chicago areas – has become increasingly unsafe over the years and is today considered 'one of the hottest areas around' (ibid.:99) by local police with one violent crime for every ten residents: 'A booming informal economy in illicit drugs has replaced the formal commercial economy that once supported the neighbourhood, and the violent conflicts among youth dealers and gang-bangers who battle for territory and market share have made North Lawndale a dangerous region, day and night' (ibid.:98).

THE CRIME-VULNERABILITY EQUATION

Gathering accounts of residents reporting that 'safety is a major issue' (ibid.:101), Klinenberg asks members of the community if the increase in violent crime has changed the way they go about their everyday. His respondent Darcy Baker who has lived in North Lawndale for over 40 years testifies that the social life of the community has indeed been profoundly affected:

> If you were standing here [in 1995] you'd see someone selling drugs on every corner . . . . groups of people . . . There were dealers standing in front of your home, hiding drugs in the yard [. . .] There were bullets coming down our block. You couldn't sit out any longer. We used to sit outside all night and just talk and do whatever. But that's changed. (ibid.)

Klinenberg's interviewees frequently confirm a strong fear of violent crime. In a bold methodological manoeuvre, Klinenberg combines this subjective fear of crime with Semenza's data on senior mortality to posit a causal relation regarding heat wave vulnerability. According to Klinenberg it is fear of crime that led to the social isolation of elderly people and ultimately to their death during the heat wave. Elderly people in North Lawndale died in large numbers *because* they were afraid of violent crime:

[Crime] undermines the basis for the kinds of collective life that might have protected isolated residents from the heat [. . .] Living with fear and organising one's routines around it, is a consequence of residing in high-crime areas with violent drug markets in the streets and a degraded public infrastructure. The impact of proximity to violence is particularly acute for the elderly, who are not only susceptible to street crime, but also vulnerable to serious physical injury as a consequence of an attack. (ibid.)

To close the gap between a perceived fear of crime and an actual increase in crime that may have contributed to the social isolation of seniors, Klinenberg draws on police data and on contemporary sociology. In 1995, Chicago ranked fifth of all American cities in aggravated assault and in 1998 it topped the list of US homicides (Klinenberg 2002:55). Just one week before the heat wave, Chicago experienced a marked homicide spike, with as many as 24 people killed in one week, provoking the *Chicago Tribune* to quip: 'City Murders on Rise with the Thermometer' (cited in ibid.), a journalistic hunch that Klinenberg seeks to confirm sociologically. Reporting that most of the murder victims were concentrated in Chicago's predominantly African American South Side, Klinenberg argues:

The same areas produced an inordinate number of heat-wave-related deaths the next week. Though they [the seniors] were unlikely targets for the shootings, older residents of violent areas who refused to leave their homes during the heat wave had reason to be concerned about the risks they faced in the city streets [. . .] Social avoidance and reclusion have become essential protective strategies for city residents whose concentration in high-crime neighbourhoods places them directly in harm's way. (ibid.:55, 58)

Citing social-psychological reports on social isolation among the elderly (Thompson and Krause 1998), Klinenberg suggests that Chicago seniors in high-crime neighbourhoods developed a 'bunker mentality', practically living in conditions of 'self-imposed house arrest' and only leaving their premises when absolutely necessary. For Klinenberg, this fear of crime led urban seniors to disregard the most elementary precautions during a heat wave. For fear of burglary, seniors kept their doors and windows tightly shut. 'In an environment where preying on the elderly is a standard and recurrent practice of neighbourhood deviants' (Klinenberg 2002:58), they didn't seek help for fear of being mugged or assaulted on the street or in public housing corridors.

THE BETTER SIBLING

However, the clearest formulation of Klinenberg's equation between crime and disaster vulnerability appears when he directly contrasts the derelict social networks of North Lawndale with the bustling social life of its southern sibling. South Lawndale or 'Little Village' experienced a different post-war development than its derelict northern neighbour. Populated by Czechoslovakian and German immigrants around the turn of the century, the community attracted many Latino and Mexican migrants to work in the same industries as blacks did, who migrated to North Lawndale. However, the two neighbourhoods were differently subjected to the deindustrialisation that began in the 1960s. While residents in North Lawndale moved out en masse, Mexican migrants kept coming to South Lawndale and developed a bustling local service sector. Additionally, home ownership in Little Village was at 36% much higher than in North Lawndale, where it didn't exceed 16%, which further prevented residents from moving out. The population surge, dense inhabitation, large family networks and buoyant local markets create a landscape in strong contrast with Klinenberg's description of North Lawndale:

> The empty lots and abandoned buildings so prevalent in the African American area give way to dense concentrations of busy sidewalks, active commerce and residential buildings packed with more inhabitants than they can hold [. . .] Whereas the social morphology of North Lawndale undermines the collective life of the area, the material substratum of busy streets, dense residential concentration, proximate family habitation, and booming commerce in Little Village fosters public activity and informal social support among area residents. (2002:109)

Klinenberg describes how the animated social life in Little Village helped produce a very low crime rate, three times lower than that of North Lawndale. The safety of the streets allows for much walking and neighbourly exchange, which helps the elderly stay fit and connected. While there are some local gangs, they mostly stick to themselves. Pro-social behaviour is common, resulting in low fear levels and a high degree of sociality. Klinenberg concludes that because of its low crime rate, this close-knit neighbourhood was much better equipped to deal with the heat than its high-crime sibling:

> In North Lawndale the dangerous ecology of abandoned buildings, open spaces, commercial depletion, violent crime, degraded infrastructure, low population density and family dispersion undermines the viability of public life and the strength of local support systems, rendering older residents particularly vulnerable to isolation. In Little Village though, the busy streets, heavy commercial activity, residential concentration, and relatively low crime promote social contact, collective life and public engagement [. . .] During the heat wave, these local conditions directly affected residents of the two community areas by constraining (North Lawndale) or creating (in Little Village) the possibility for social contact that helped vulnerable Chicagoans to survive. (ibid.:91)

Klinenberg's argument is as simple as it is effective. Vulnerability is produced by the criminal degradation of urban civic life. This breakdown is triggered by external factors, such as governmental neglect and high unemployment, but also significantly, by the internal spread of urban crime and its permeation of community life. In Little Village, crime was limited by the existence of healthy social networks and a vibrant public life. In North Lawndale, it was granted free reign due to a defunct infrastructure, a population without perspective and the absence of a legal job market.

How convincing is crime as a causal factor for senior mortality during the heat wave? According to fellow sociologist Mitchell Duneier, not very much. In a critical commentary, Duneier takes issue with Klinenberg's selection of North Lawndale and South Lawndale as comparative sites to analyse heat wave mortality. While the two neighbourhoods are comparable with respect to seniors living alone and seniors living in poverty, Klinenberg himself initially remarks on the striking difference in the overall poverty rate between the two areas. Thus, in North Lawndale, 44 per cent of residents live below the poverty line, while in South Lawndale it is only 22 per cent (Duneier, 2004:141). Adding the variable of median household income to the data pool, Duneier shows that South Lawndale has an average household income of $22,260, compared to North Lawndale's $12,570 (ibid.). In his analysis, however, Klinenberg skims over this chasm in average neighbourhood wealth and instead focusses his attention on race and crime as determining mortality factors. Duneier is perplexed at the omission of such a crucial mortality variable, remarking that:

> Given the strong links between poverty and health vulnerability, it would seem that the significant economic differences between the two communities could explain death rate differentials without resort to ethnicity or still more subtle ecological factors [. . .] North Lawndale is twice as poor as South Lawndale. The African Americans in North Lawndale had fewer economic resources and could not afford air conditioners as easily or lacked the wherewithal to aid their elderly kin and friends, compared to those living in the relatively better off Latino neighborhood. (ibid.:141, 146–7)

For Duneier, taking the striking difference in neighbourhood incomes into account, there is no need to resort to crime as an additional causal element. Income alone, and its strong correlation with health, are sufficient reasons to explain the Lawndale's stark mortality difference. Duneier's intervention severely challenges Klinenberg's methodological accuracy, dismissing the two neighbourhoods as largely incomparable. Pace Klinenberg's own assurances to the contrary, Duneier reproaches Klinenberg of a hidden racial prejudice, concluding that:

> Instead of writing ambiguously about the 'cultural dispositions' of Latinos, the fragmented families of blacks, Klinenberg [could] have told a more compelling story about the significant forces that are leading families of all races to become fragmented, leaving their elders to die alone. [This] failure amounts to an inexplicable and apparently baseless racial comparison. (ibid.:143)

VULNERABILITY FROM THE STANDPOINT OF SOCIAL REPRODUCTION

Reviewing the sociological literature on the Chicago Heat Wave, we are left with two possible scenarios to explain elevated senior mortality: High crime and pervasive senior poverty. Rather than evaluate the plausibility of either explanation or add my own, I want to zoom out and look at both diagnoses from the standpoint of social reproduction. When seen in light of social reproduction, both diagnoses give us important insights into the social-reproductive crisis that permeated not only Chicago in the 1990s but the entirety of the Reagan and Clinton years. Leaving sociological quibbles about the comparability of distinct Chicago neighbourhoods by the wayside, we can in this way tell a 'more compelling story', not merely of the factors that led to seniors dying alone in the Chicago Heat Wave, but of the social forces that impoverished the elderly and led the young to commit crimes in the 1980s and 1990s. Studying disaster in this way opens up to a broader analysis of social reproduction in a given historical period.

In the following, I will explain the increase in senior poverty and the rise in crime from within the particular configuration of production and social reproduction in the late twentieth century. Doing so will shed light on the appearance of both vulnerability factors as the differential effects of austerity, following mid-century deindustrialisation. While these factors make populations vulnerable to the effects of natural disaster, what is more important is that they erode the conditions of these populations' everyday lives. Rather than asking what social factors contribute to disaster vulnerability, we should ask the opposite question: What does disaster vulnerability show us about everyday lives lived in crisis? While disaster studies diagnoses distinct vulnerability factors that negatively affect a population's capacity to cope with calamity, a social reproduction approach to disaster broadens disaster studies' analyses to a wider and more deep-seated examination of social crises. When considering senior poverty and rising crime from the standpoint of social reproduction, we gain a wider picture of the ways in which the predicament of the young and the old changed in the 1980s. Let us begin with the elderly.

OLD AGE POVERTY

Politicians and social scientists first became aware of the alarming increase in old-age poverty in the early 1960s through a nationwide survey of senior citizen income, organised by the US Senate, and through the 1961 White House Conference on Aging. In his landmark study from 1962, *The other America*, sociologist Michael Harrington synthesised the results of the governmental surveys into a book-length warning about the corrosive effects of old-age poverty. While senior poverty was low in the 1950s, the 1960s witnessed a drastic increase in seniors living in destitution. As Harrington writes:

The 1960 Senate report stated the issue clearly enough: '. . . at least one-half of the aged – approximately eight million people – cannot afford today decent housing, proper nutrition, adequate medical care, preventive or acute, or necessary recreation.' The same grim picture emerged from the White House Conference on Aging in 1961. As one volume put it, 'Many states report that half their citizens over 65 have incomes too low to meet their basic needs'. (1962:104)

After the economic boom of the 1950s, how did this come to pass? According to Harrington, the increase in old-age poverty was a home-grown phenomenon of demographic developments in industrial societies. Advances in medicine and nutrition enabled the population to live much longer than at the turn of the century. While mortality rates were decreasing, fertility rates were similarly declining, leading to an increasingly skewed balance between pension recipients and pension contributors. Furthermore, immigration, formerly a strong factor in population growth, had been scaled back. Taken together, these factors led to an overall aging of the population.[30] Instead of looking at senior poverty in isolation, Harrington is keen to point to the reproduction of poverty across the lifetime from youth to old age as one integrated process:

This is no country for old men. The physical humiliation and the loneliness are real, but to them is added the indignity of living in a society that is obsessed by youth and tries to ignore age. These people are caught [. . .] in a triple 'chain of causality': they are plagued by ill health; they do not have enough money; and they are socially isolated [. . .] A good many are old and poor because they were young and poor, middle-aged and poor. (ibid.:102)

In a classical Marxist gesture, Harrington embeds senior poverty in the general poverty trends of all age groups. It is therefore not that seniors are specifically poor. Rather, poor seniors are the result of a lifetime lived in poverty. In this view, old-age poverty appears as an effect of the overall reproduction of class society that maintains social wealth in the hands of a small elite, at the expense of the destitute majority. Old-age poverty exemplifies the iron law of class societies, where those born into poverty will likely remain poor.

How does this reproduction of class and its associated wealth levels operate throughout a human being's lifetime? Aiming to write a political economy of old age, the social gerontologist Alan Walker provides an analysis that is firmly rooted in the labour market. According to Walker, different social classes have an unequal access to society's economic resources, specifically to labour, as a source of income during their lifetime. According to their position on the job market, they are more or less securely employed, with more or less money to invest in preparing for old age in the form of savings, insurances and capital assets. For Walker, the main criterion for old-age poverty is an individual's position on the job market, which in turn, is conditioned by their class position:

> During working life differential access is granted to social systems which distribute resources, the most important of which is employment. Those with high incomes from employment are more likely than others to accumulate savings, property and private pension rights [. . .] Those wholly or predominantly excluded from the labour market, including people with disabilities and some women, are most likely to be amongst the very poorest in old age. (2008:76–7)

While structurally sound, this class-based argument cannot explain why, since the 1960s, the number of poor seniors has steadily continued to rise, with one in five elderly Americans living below the poverty line by the 1980s (Walker, 2008:74). We therefore need a more dynamic account of old-age poverty that can explain the particular increase in senior poverty since the 1960s. I suggest that this account starts from the rapid fall in the demand for labour power with the decline of American heavy industry, the ensuing growth of the social category of 'the retired' and the gradual financialisation of pensions.

In the reconstruction years following WWII, there was a general shortage of manual labour, since the second heyday of industrialisation, driven by automobiles and consumer electronics absorbed a huge amount of labour power. At this time, the elderly were actively discouraged from retiring, since their labour power was dearly needed. As Alan Walker specifies, 'these frequent appeals [for seniors to stay in employment] were accompanied and part legitimated by a body of academic and medical evidence stressing the detrimental effects of retirement' (ibid.:84). Indeed, while physically taxing, industrial employment and trade union membership created meaningful links for aging workers to a lively social universe at the workplace and beyond.

When, beginning in the 1960s, industrial markets became increasingly saturated and American production began to be moved offshore, the demand for manual labour dropped, and with it, the need for workers to stay in employment during old age. This led to a lowering of the statutory retirement age in almost all industrial countries, and therefore to a numerical increase in citizens, counting as 'seniors'. Alan Walker outlines how the socially constructed category of 'the elderly' became a growing feature of industrial societies:

> It is important to establish at the outset that 'old' age is socially defined, as the statutory retirement age. In a relatively short space of time, retirement has become a dominant social process in the lives of older people. This trend can be illustrated simply by reference to successive cohorts of those currently over retirement age. Four-fifths of those elderly people living in the community who are aged 85 and over continued working for some period after the statutory retirement age, compared with one-half of those aged from 75 to 84 and just over one-third of those aged 65–74. (ibid.:81)

Old age is thus a mobile category, closely tied to the statutory retirement age, which in turn is tied to the demand for labour power. As the demand for labour fell with deindustrialisation, the number of seniors rose, as more and more elderly people were ejected from employment. Both what counts as old age and the way it is lived are therefore dependent on the development of industry and capital at a given historical moment. If we keep in mind, with Walker, that retiring 'results in an average fall in income of about one-half' (ibid.), it becomes clear why the 1970s and 1980s, with their tendential drop in the demand for labour power, witnessed such a drastic increase in old-age poverty. Since the economic crisis continued unabated after the late 1960s, and since the demand for labour diminished with it, the overall number of seniors, as well as the number of seniors living in poverty have steadily increased as social phenomena.

To absorb this demographic aging of the population, the pension system in over 30 countries has been fundamentally reformed between the 1970s and the 1990s, lessening the historical involvement of the state and heightening the involvement of the market in order to save on state-led social reproduction. This development has led to a further tightening of the financial screw for working class pensioners. To fully understand these changes, let us first ask what a pension actually is. It is common sense to think of pensions as an insurance system that provides for aging workers, once they have lost their ability to work. Akin to a savings account, a worker pays a portion of their salary into a pension fund throughout their active life as an employee. After retirement, this money is paid out to the employee as a form of delayed wage payment. In this view, pensions are rooted in the production process, comprising an active phase and a passive phase. In the active phase, the worker sells their labour power in exchange for a wage. While most of this wage is used for the worker's immediate reproduction, a portion of it is withheld and paid into a pension fund. In the passive phase, commencing with retirement, the worker is paid out this portion of their salary to enable their reproduction in the absence of a wage.

In this view, pensions are entirely a by-product of capitalist production, in which compensation for one's labour occurs through wages in the worker's active life and through pensions in the worker's passive life. However, this only tells us what happens to the worker at the individual level. If we abstract from the individual plane and see pensions through their role within social reproduction, rather than production, we can conceptualise them not as an individual but as an intergenerational phenomenon.

Recall that for social reproduction theorists, capitalist production is always made possible by a set of background conditions. These background conditions involve the reproduction of labour power that ensures there is a fresh supply of workers available to capitalist production every day. In the words of political theorist Nancy Fraser, social reproduction theory adopts: 'An expanded understanding of capitalism, encompassing both its official economy and the latter's non-economic background conditions [. . .] Capitalism's economic subsystem depends on social-reproductive activities external to it, which form one of its background conditions of possibility' (2017:23).

These background conditions are vital, since, as Fraser points out, it is generally not capitalists who pay for the reproduction of labour power. Instead, the reproductive burden is shared between families, who perform the biological urform of social reproduction in the rearing of children and the preparation of meals, and the sophisticated reproductive services of the state, such as education, health care and pensions. It is only in this expanded view, that pensions appear in their full significance as an investment into the intergenerational reproduction of workers under capitalism. Since kin-based support systems increasingly broke away under capitalism, the state historically expanded to fill the gaps that capitalist development tore into the social fabric. Pensions emerged with the development of the working class as that segment of the population that depends entirely on the wage for its subsistence. For the economist Serap Saritas Oran: 'Pensions are a component of the broader understanding of the value of labour power as a standard of living of the working class that consists of payments and benefits necessary for generational social reproduction' (2017:149).

Pensions in this view become a battlefield of social reproduction. Their level is determined in the crossfire between capital and labour to determine the value of labour power at a given point in history. While they became a state-run reproductive service in an industrial world that had a seemingly unappeasable thirst for labour, when this thirst was quenched by the 1970s, the state gradually withdrew from the provision of pensions, since they now appeared as a mere cost. The result was a large-scale pension reform that shifted the burden of reproducing the elderly from the state back onto individuals and communities.

Since their broad implementation in the early twentieth century until the 1980s, pensions were generally financed through a public pay-as-you-go or defined-benefit scheme. In defined-benefit schemes, employees are promised a pension, based on their salary level and length of employment. While workers pay a portion of their salary into a pension fund, another portion is paid by the employer. In addition, the state supplements the accrued pension revenue through returns from general income tax. Born when the cost of labour was dear, this system is employee-friendly, since it makes employers responsible to pay the pensions of their employees according to a pre-defined formula. Furthermore, it is redistributive, since tax levels are income dependent. In this way, under defined-benefit schemes, the wealthy contribute to the pensions of the poor.

In the 1980s however, under increasing fears of an aging population, the defined-benefit schemes were increasingly replaced with financialised or so-called defined-contribution schemes. This meant that rather than the state being the arbiter of pension funds, the accumulated pension capital was now invested in financial markets, supposedly to absorb the increasing imbalance between pension contributors and pension recipients. In 1994, the International Monetary Fund's report *Averting the Old-Age Crisis*, laid out the ideology behind the marketisation of pensions. As Oran summarises: 'According to the report, the world population is aging; the best way to cope with budget deficits related to the increasing number of retirees (compared to workers) is to privatize state pensions and leave pension provision to the market' (2017:162).

Irrespective of their alleged social value, the marketisation of pensions created above all financial value, as markets were flooded with investors' pension money. Today, national, as well as private pension funds are big financial players, investing heavily in banking, real estate, and natural resources. In the new financialised schemes, pensions cease to depend on a worker's salary level and length of employment. Instead, employees choose a pension fund to pay into during their working years. After retirement, their pension level depends on the market performance of their fund-of-choice. Born at a time of deindustrialisation when the price of labour was cheap and unions' bargaining power in tatters, financialised pensions are employer-friendly, since they make employees responsible for making smart investment decisions on a competitive market. In case their fund doesn't perform, or an economic crisis hits, only the worker carries the financial risk of a drop in pensions. Thus, workers who retired after the 2008 financial crisis that swept away much of the wealth of US pension funds, lost out to market forces, even after a lifetime of carefully weighing their investment options. As Oran further explains:

> In the case of a funded scheme, even though the worker contributes for years, the return depends on the circumstances of the financial markets. Therefore, a pensioner who retires right after a huge financial crisis is just *unlucky* for accruing half of the pension benefit she was expecting before [. . .] There is no one to blame for bad management [. . .] The authorities might even accuse the pensioner of investing in risky assets. (ibid.:164)

While public defined pension schemes represented the state's attempt to distribute the cost of generational social reproduction through taxes on income, financialised pensions go the opposite way. Part and parcel of the spate of austerity measures that hit the US in the 1980s, financialised pensions shift the reproductive burden away from the state and capital and back onto communities and workers. Against the lofty expectations of the International Monetary Fund however, financialising pensions did not lead to a golden age of retiree prosperity. Instead, we have seen a steep drop in pension levels since the introduction of financialised models. Even the liberal *Economist* confirms that: 'Many employees face retirement with an income well short of their expectations. An employee who pays into a DC [direct-contribution] scheme for 40 years may only get half the retirement income he could have expected under a final-salary system' (2008: para. 2).

Regardless of the predicted loss in income, the policy shift has continued unabated since the 1980s. While in 1979, 62% of US private sector employees were insured via direct-benefit pension plans and only 17% through financialised plans, by 2009, these figures had reversed to only 7% covered through direct-benefit schemes and 68% covered by financialised plans (ibid.). However, even in case of an economic boom, such as during the bull market of the 1990s, pension gains will be contingent upon prior investment choices. Financialised schemes favour high and middle-income earners, who are permanently employed, able to consistently pay into pension funds, and who possess the means and the leisure to hedge their bets on the pension market. This explains why, during the heyday of finance capital in the 1990s, high earners benefitted from financialised schemes, while the under, or informally employed got poorer and poorer. Oran sums up the differential impact of financialised pensions:

> Recent pension reforms have exacerbated the social-reproduction-related problems of disadvantaged groups within the working class, such as workers who are employed occasionally and those who are employed informally. Those vulnerable groups benefited from the redistributive mechanism of PAYG state schemes in the past. However, with individual funded schemes, it is hard for these groups to gain access to adequate pension income. (2017:165)

We therefore face a huge and home-grown production of old-age poverty as the result of the growth of surplus populations, following deindustrialisation, the demographic aging of the population, and the neoliberal attacks on formerly state-funded domains of social reproduction, such as pensions. At 21.5 per cent, the US has the third highest senior poverty levels of any OECD country (OECD, 2013:165). While old age poverty may explain why so many seniors died during the Chicago Heat Wave, it represents a catastrophe in its own right. While we are accustomed to thinking about the misery of surplus populations during youth and working age, we tend to forget that economic crises severely affect the elderly as well. This is not only because chronic unemployment in prime working years naturally affects incomes later in life. Rather, as we have seen, deindustrialisation and its dismal effects on pensions affected the working class intergenerationally, producing a severe slump in living standards. While plausibly making the elderly more vulnerable to the effects of natural disaster, this social reproductive crisis is not captured by analyses that narrowly focus only on heat wave mortality during a calamity.

YOUTH CRIME

Let us now turn our attention to crime. I argue that the rising crime rate has its roots in the same social-reproductive crisis as senior poverty, while capturing its opposite generational pole. While fear of crime is not a very plausible factor for heat wave mortality, I suggest that Klinenberg inadvertently captures the other side of senior poverty in the phenomenon of rising crime. From a social reproduction perspective, both represent opposite ends of the reproductive crisis that followed American deindustrialisation, ejecting large numbers of Americans from the possibility of reproducing themselves through waged employment. Already in 1962 Michael Harrington linked the two phenomena, observing that: 'For the younger slum dweller there is some kind of street society, even if it takes the form of gangs. But for the old person, trapped in the decaying central area of the city and living among strangers, there is a terrifying lack of simple human contact' (1962:109).

While Klinenberg's demonisation of crime as a corrosive social ill is certainly exemplary of the conservative way of thinking about crime, a closer look at the crime statistics, assembled from a variety of sources across the political spectrum all point to a drastic increase in criminal activity between 1970 and 1990. According to the nonpartisan Brennan Center for Justice, violent crime increased by 126 per cent between 1960 and 1970 and by 67 per cent between 1970 and 1980. After a brief decline in the early 1980s, it rose again exponentially until it peaked in 1991 (Eisen and Roeder, 2015: para. 6). The federal archives from the Bureau of Justice Statistics (Cooper and Smith, 2011) and the non-governmental fact-checking organisation The Poynter Institute (Kaplan, 2017) all corroborate these trends.

Compiling crime statistics is a notoriously thorny task. For the most part, only reported crimes are recorded, while the majority of crime goes unreported. Furthermore, fear of, and over-sensitisation to crime among the police habitually leads to over-reporting and contributes to a general police bias.[31] However, also the National Crime Victimization Survey that takes police and judiciary bias into account by anonymously documenting unreported crime shows the same rise in crime from 1970 to 1991 (Rand, Lynch and Cantor, 1997:1). How does race figure in these numbers? According to the homicide rates, compiled by the Bureau of Justice Statistics, 'blacks were disproportionately represented among homicide victims and offenders' (Cooper and Smith, 2011:11). Between 1983 and 1991, both homicide victimisation and offending rates among blacks were over eight times higher than those among whites (ibid.). Crucially, a majority of these homicides were drug related. While 'black offenders are less likely to be involved in sex-related killings, workplace homicides or homicides of elders' (ibid:12), they make up two thirds (65.6%) of drug-related homicides (ibid.), making drugs the overwhelming reason why African Americans kill each other.

While conservatives, such as Klinenberg, insist on defunct family ties and corroding social networks as the causes for why African Americans were prone to crime in the 1980s and 1990s, I argue that the causes for this increase are to be found in the same mid-century changes to the American labour market that also plunged senior citizens into a deep reproductive crisis. In order to understand how the economic crisis led to a rise in black crime, we have to look at the relation between race and deindustrialisation.

It is important to point out that already before the crisis, the US economy was profoundly racially structured. Suffering the long-term consequences of slavery and segregation, blacks had only limited access to the job market until formal desegregation in the 1960s. These factors resulted in black unemployment being between 150 to 400 per cent higher than white unemployment in the years immediately following WWII (Clover, 2016b:116). Even after desegregation, racism was rampant on the factory floor. Plant managers customarily separated workers according to race to drive down wages. In the automobile plants, blacks were often confined to the foundry, carrying out the most burdensome and strenuous work (Michney, 2007:936).

While in the post-war period, white workers could meaningfully identify with labour as an essential part of their identity, blacks frequently only had tenuous links with formal work and often had to make ends meet through informal labour, including day jobs, illegal employment, and the reselling of wholesale goods.[32] Nevertheless the period immediately following desegregation represented something of a gilded decade for the black working class. Blacks migrated en masse to the northern industrial cities to find work in the steel mines and automobile plants and for a while, industrial labour accommodated the fresh influx of workers, offering high salaries to low-skilled African American workers.

Carried into the twentieth century largely by the national war economies and post-war reconstruction, American production slowly ground to a halt in the late 1960s. Major industrial cities such as Detroit and Newark began laying off workers and downsizing their output as early as 1960 (Herman, 2005:87; Sugrue, 1996:144). Scholars such as Robert Brenner (2006) and David McNally (2009) have diagnosed a 'long downturn' and 'world-slump' – setting in around 1960 and lasting until today – in which production was first moved offshore and then scaled back, resulting in skyrocketing levels of unemployment. By the 1980s, when the steel mining sector was progressively shut down, American heavy industry had shrunk to a fraction of what it had been in the early twentieth century (Schulman, 1982:33).[33] Coupled with growing automation in key industries, such as manufacture that made labour increasingly redundant, this slowdown led to more and more people being ejected from formal employment. The Bureau of Labour Statistics show that between 1980 and 2000, two million manufacturing jobs were lost in this way (Hernandez, 2018:1). According to a paper by the National Bureau of Economic Research, this downsizing led to 'a ten percentage point decline in the local manufacturing share [that] reduced local employment rates by 3.7 percentage points for prime age men and 2.7 percentage points for prime age women' (Charles, Hurst and Schwartz, 2018:2).

The slowdown of the productive economy was experienced particularly harshly by the black population that had only just managed to find a toehold in American heavy industry. Known as 'last hired, first fired', black workers were often the first to be laid off when industrial companies downsized their production. Research by the Economic Policy Institute further shows that the average salary of black men who managed to stay in employment dropped much more drastically than the average salary of white men. While the Trump campaign made much out of the growing immiseration of white Americans, the figures show that between 1979 and 2015 'median hourly wages of black men

fell by 5.7 per cent compared with a 1.0 per cent decline for white men'
(Wilson, 2016:5). When production stalled with deindustrialisation,
blacks again found themselves increasingly excluded from the labour
market.

An immediate effect of this growing exclusion from formal waged
employment was the growth of the informal economy, particularly the
drug trade. If blacks are perpetually excluded from waged employment,
they must find other ways to survive, and the illegal, informal economy
is one of these ways. We shouldn't be surprised that, if black unemployment grows, so does the informal economy and therefore the crime rate,
the rate at which people are doing things the state designates as illegal.
In this perspective, the mid-century rise in crime becomes legible as a
direct result of American deindustrialisation. Endnotes have recently
captured this development, arguing that:

> As the regulation of social relations by the labour market began to
> break down with the slowing of the economy, proletarians were
> ejected from the industrial sector, leading to rising unemployment
> and under-employment, and growth in low-wage services. Popula-
> tions fled towards suburbs, leaving behind decaying inner cities. [. . .]
> Communities that were supposed to achieve autonomy in the context
> of the Black Power Movement found themselves riven with crime and
> desperation. (2015a:64–5)

Rather than building autonomous structures, as the Black Panthers
envisioned it, black populations found themselves isolated and underem-
ployed with the advent of deindustrialisation. Instead of, like Klinenberg,
locating the cause of crime in 'cultural dispositions' or 'fragmented
families', the reasons for the rise in crime are to be found in the historical
unfolding of deindustrialisation that overrode the political gains, won by
the Civil Rights Movement. In cities such as St. Louis, Missouri, many
neighbourhoods are 95% black and have an unemployment rate of 50%
(Endnotes, 2015:32) It is coherent that in conditions of such rampant
unemployment, people turn to the informal drug economy as a means to
generate income. Since this economy lacks the legal and judicial protec-
tions that still characterise the formal economy, transactions often have
to be underwritten by direct force. Carrying a gun is simply part of the
job description.

Further support for this materialist explanation of crime is provided by the fact that, as the 2008 economic crisis finally began to also gnaw at the wealth of white Americans, white crime rates too drastically increased. This is reflected in recent incarceration trends. Since the onset of the crisis, between 1970 and 2000, black and white incarceration rates have risen at around the same speed. From the year 2000 onwards however, the white incarceration rate continued to rise, even as blacks began to be less frequently incarcerated (Endnotes, 2015a:31). To be sure, blacks are still jailed in far higher total numbers, but the difference between white and black incarceration rates is actually decreasing. As Endnotes further point out: 'Even if every black man currently in jail were miraculously set free, in a sort of anti-racist rapture, the US would still have the highest incarceration rate in the world (ibid.).'

These statistics point to class, rather than race, as a main determinant for criminal activity. Historically, since poverty rates have always been much higher for black Americans, black crime rates have tended to be higher, with a predictable spike in times of economic crisis. However, as the crisis also increasingly ejected white Americans from the privilege of waged work, white crime rates too began to rise.

In summary, analyses from disaster studies, such as Klinenberg's and Duneier's narrow accounts of old-age vulnerability fall short of grasping the real historical conditions that led to seniors dying destitute and youth joining gangs in the 1990s. While naively relating one to the other in a chain of causality, Klinenberg fails to see senior vulnerability and youth crime as parallel effects of the crisis in social reproduction that followed American deindustrialisation. If we see them as isolated social facts, leading to death during disaster, senior poverty and high youth crime cannot be grasped in their deep, historical significance. When considered in light of the retrenchment of the state-led social reproduction on the other hand, both phenomena become legible as the differential effects of austerity on the lifetime of the black working class from youth to old age.

With communities suffering the effects of persistent economic crisis, civil society organising was visibly in crisis in the 1990s. After the turn of the millennium, however, the financial crisis of 2008 set off vehement anti-austerity protests around the world. While the Arab Spring sought to shake loose the shackles of American-backed regional dictators, protests quickly spread to the West with the UK and US student demonstrations forming the middle-class counterpart to the Tottenham and

Oakland riots. In New York, one of the largest recent social movements, Occupy Wall Street successfully took over Zuccotti Park in Lower Manhattan to protest the federal bailout of US banks. What was less talked about during this wave of insurrection was that the self-organised social movement would soon become a major force in a new model of disaster relief that would reconfigure the roles of the state and civil society yet again.

7

2012: The Strange Success of Occupy Sandy

Somebody's gotta be there when it gets ugly
Somebody's gotta be there when it gets bloody
Somebody's gotta get their hands dirty
Yo, it's a fucked up job but somebody's gotta do it
— The Roots

THE MOMENT OF OCCUPY SANDY

It is Thursday, 8 November 2012 at St. Jacobi Church in Sunset Park, Brooklyn; a bright, dry day. Just one week earlier, Hurricane Sandy made landfall on the East Coast, ravaging everything in its wake. In New York City, thousands of houses are destroyed or flooded. Thousands of households in the low-lying areas of Staten Island, Red Hook and the Rockaways are still without electricity. At St. Jacobi Church, young people with smartphones and walkie-talkies are sifting through piles of donations, sorting canned food, diapers, torches, candles, bed covers and power generators into stacks and loading them onto trucks. A young man with a scruffy-looking beard posts on Facebook: 'Attention! If anyone in Rockaway needs to have their basement pumped, please contact Suzanne Hamalak at suzybklyn@aol.com. Her family wants to help and have industrial pumps [...] they will do it for free' (cited in Barr, 2012: para. 10). The young man is part of Occupy Sandy, Occupy Wall Street's disaster relief agency that set up camp in Brooklyn a day after the hurricane, while the Red Cross and FEMA were still struggling to get personnel out to New York's hardest-hit areas.

The most lethal and destructive hurricane of the 2012 Atlantic hurricane season, Sandy's immediate death toll in New York City alone was 97, followed by weeks-long power cuts and billions of dollars in damage (Schmeltz, González et al., 2013:799). Sandy revealed the staggering vulnerability of low-lying New York City areas that proved incapable of protecting themselves. While low-lying areas are naturally vulnerable to flooding, this vulnerability was exacerbated by drastic economic and social factors. Red Hook, one of the hardest-hit neighbourhoods in Brooklyn, has a 45% poverty rate with soaring levels of asthma and diabetes (Brockwell, Kilminster et al., 2009:20). While many wealthy Manhattaners and residents on higher ground experienced virtually no disruption to their everyday, the devastation wrought by Sandy on the lower-lying parts of the city was extreme, as the journalist Nick Pinto describes:

> Power was out in huge swaths. Flooded tunnels cut off whole regions from the rest of the city. In Lower Manhattan, Red Hook, Coney Island, the Rockaways, and much of Staten Island, everything from electricity to heat to potable water was in short supply. Hospitals were being evacuated after power failures. Bodies drowned in the storm surge were being recovered. The news media began to show the first images of Breezy Point, burned to the ground, and houses up and down the coast torn apart by wind and water. (2012: para. 1)

In ghostly reminiscence of Hurricane Katrina, it quickly became clear that the relief efforts of the Federal Emergency Management Agency (FEMA) and the Red Cross were inadequate.[34] While FEMA's contingency plans had 'anticipated aftereffects such as electrical fires, flooding, and displacement of populations residing in evacuation zones' (Schmeltz, González et al., 2013:800), the emergency planners did not expect that the power cuts would entail a crucial lack of services, affecting everything from clean drinking water and sanitation to food provision. Furthermore, the concentration of emergency personnel on Lower Manhattan neglected those outlying boroughs that were worst hit by the flooding: 'They put a lot of attention to Lower Manhattan when they should have been in Coney Island' (cited in Feeney, 2012: para. 2), said the exhausted volunteer Nick Weissman of Williamsburg.

Part of the failure of the Red Cross and of FEMA to adequately address the situation on the ground can be attributed to the emergency managers' disconnect from local communities. While there existed numerous contingency and hazard adaptation plans such as PlaNYC from the Office of the Mayor and the New York City Hazard Mitigation Plan from the NYC Office for Emergency Management, official schemes tended to be technocratic and did not integrate the local level of community organising.[35] Thus, while FEMA does train community response teams to enact hazard mitigation in their neighbourhoods, these community responders are not integrated into adaptation and mitigation planning committees, creating a communication lag between local and central levels of administration (Schmeltz, González et al., 2013:802). In the aftermath of Sandy, this 'aid gap', left by the official relief workers, set the stage for the volunteer-based relief work of *Occupy Sandy*, activists from the social movement Occupy Wall Street that had occupied Zuccotti Park in Lower Manhattan to protest American austerity politics a few months prior to Sandy and were now looking for a new mission.

Tapping into the existing social media network of *Occupy*, the activists quickly set up camp in Brooklyn, utilising Twitter to call for manpower and donations. It soon turned out that social media was quicker and more effective than waiting for official aid workers to be deployed. As Nick Weissman specified: 'Occupy Sandy had Twitter feeds running and a community kitchen set up by Tuesday night after the storm, whereas larger organisations, with bigger bureaucracies, were unable to respond as quickly and specifically' (cited in Feeney, 2012: para. 2).

In only a short space of time, Occupy responded by providing tens of thousands of volunteers (four times the number of official aid workers), an estimated 15,000 meals and 120 truckloads of essential supplies (Kilkenny, 2013: para. 2), whilst raising $1.5 million in donations (Maslin, 2013: para. 2). Donors were sympathetic to Occupy's hands-on approach, often preferring to give to the social movement rather than to the Red Cross' 'comparatively sluggish response' (ibid.: para. 18). By February 2013, Occupy Sandy's track record was even more impressive, as the journalist Sam Knight chronicled:

> In February 2013, the group claimed to have filled 27,000 meal requests and reported assisting 3,400 residents with medical help, financial assistance, repairs and basic supplies with a mere $1.34 million – roughly 1 percent of the entire Red Cross payroll and less than the sum of three Red Cross executives' salaries in 2012. (2014: para. 20)

Faced with the paucity of the official aid effort, Occupy Sandy quickly gained public as well as media favour. Time and again, journalists and commentators compared the effectiveness of Occupy's bottom-up organising to the inertia of the official aid organisations. Likening the federal failure to deliver fast and effective relief to FEMA's negligence during Hurricane Katrina, Nick Pinto commented:

> As temperatures dropped toward freezing two weeks after the storm, residents in public-housing apartments from Red Hook to the Lower East Side to Rockaway were still without power, water, and heat. Displaced homeowners surveyed the wreckage of their lives and wondered how they'd ever build back. And almost everywhere, the vaunted presence of FEMA and the Red Cross was next to invisible. Weeks after the storm, many New Yorkers in storm-damaged neighborhoods had yet to see any sort of institutional relief at all. (2012: para. 4)

Occupy capitalised on this failure and made the independence from slow and ineffective government into one of its hallmarks. Mike Birch, one of Occupy's many cooks, championed this direct-action approach when interviewed by a reporter from *Voice of America*: 'Grassroots, real people power. We don't rely on the Red Cross, or FEMA, or the city' (cited in Weaver, 2012: para. 18). Surveying the situation on the ground, the news report praised the unparalleled efficiency of Occupy's relief effort: 'The scene at St. Jacobi Church, Brooklyn is controlled chaos: scores of people sorting and distributing tons of aid for relief centres in the hardest-hit parts of New York. Everyone is a volunteer, and all seem to be working at top speed' (ibid.: para. 1).

Occupy Sandy proved what is proven time and again in disasters from New Orleans to the Philippines to Porte-au-Prince. Namely, that self-organised citizen initiatives are better first responders to calamities than large governmental bodies. Among the first to note this fact was pioneering disaster scholar Charles Fritz, who in the 1960s, observed the communitarian behaviour that disasters generally inspire and rejected the frequent media reports of social collapse as the stuff of disaster movies:[36]

> Even under the worst disaster conditions, people maintain or quickly regain self control and become concerned about the welfare of others. Most of the initial search, rescue, and relief activities are undertaken by disaster victims before the arrival of organized outside aid. Reports of looting in disasters are grossly exaggerated; rates of theft and burglary actually decline in disasters; and much more is given

away than stolen. Other forms of antisocial behaviour, such as aggression toward others and scapegoating, are rare or nonexistent. Instead, most disasters produce a great increase in social solidarity among the stricken populace. (1996:10)

Occupy's self-organised aid effort confirms the decades-long promotion of *local knowledge* in disaster studies. Criticising the cold-war understanding of disasters as natural contingencies or technical failures, disaster studies began endorsing so-called 'local' methods of disaster risk reduction after its vulnerability turn in the 1970s. Rather than proposing a short-term fix, delivered by the momentary presence of aid workers or military personnel, the vulnerability approach promoted local knowledge as the answer to natural and man-made hazards. In doing so, it broke with the technocratic emphasis on expert knowledge that had dominated disaster research after WWII. How did vulnerability studies frame the idea of *local* as compared to *expert* knowledge?

VULNERABILITY AND THE EMERGENCE OF LOCAL KNOWLEDGE

In the 1970s, disaster scholars rejected the emphasis on expert authority that had dominated the disaster sector in the post-war era. With the awareness that disasters were not simply natural occurrences but socially produced, came a sensitivity for the local, cultural context that had given rise to a disaster, heightened its intensity, or mitigated its destructive effects. Here's how disaster scholar Kathleen Tierney defines the turn towards vulnerability: 'Put simply, the organizing idea [. . .] is that disasters and their impacts are socially produced, and that the forces driving the production of disaster are embedded in the social order itself' (2014:4).

Rather than proposing a short-term fix, delivered by the momentary presence of aid workers, the vulnerability approach began promoting 'local knowledge' as the answer to disaster risk reduction. Organising aid in a top-down way, the technocratic approach had ignored established ways of responding to hazards. Since it framed disaster victims through a matrix of scientific expertise that denied them any access to relevant knowledge, as well as to the resources needed to organise the relief effort, victims and survivors were simply not listened to. In the words of vulnerability scholars Blaikie, Wisner, Cannon and Davis:

Too often, survivors are relegated to the role of passive spectators by aid workers who rapidly take over the entire recovery process [. . .] Some international consultants and the staff of certain agencies tend to sprout like mushrooms after disasters that attract media coverage [. . .] Such officials typically do their job and then all too quickly depart from the scene for yet another disaster or administrative talk or commission. (1994:207, 214)

Since the technocratic approach had derided local knowledge as ineffective in the fight against hazards, vulnerability scholars' strategy lay in radically changing the valence of local knowledge, which now emerged as the primary solution to building disaster resilience. Critical of the technocratic approach's top-down authoritarianism, vulnerability studies recognised that communities afflicted by disaster mostly already possessed the resources needed for an effective response. Since disasters frequently reoccur in specific regions of the world, vulnerability scholars trust local people to have acquired the capacity and the skills for an adequate response.

Such local capacities include various elements in a community's way of life, for example, technologies such as informal security systems, elaborate practices of land use and ecosystems management, adapted to the risk of floods, storms or drought. For vulnerability scholars, these practices constitute a learnt habitus, perfectly adapted to a particular environment with its own dangers and risks. The vulnerability approach reserves a minimal role to aid workers, whose task is reduced to bringing local knowledge to the fore to act as its facilitators. Rather than as a technocratic expert, it views aid workers as cultural coordinators, trained in reading those local capacities that might at first sight be illegible to an outsider. For Greg Bankoff:

The current emphasis on the importance of [. . .] local knowledge in disaster situations is a belated recognition that [people] have historically developed sophisticated strategies and complex institutions to reduce the constant insecurity of their lives [. . .] The respect now accorded to coping practices forms part of a wider attempt to broaden local participation in the entire development process through bottom-up planning and to empower local people through encouraging community participation. Local knowledge is seen as the key to success as it is the only resource controlled by the most vulnerable, is already present at a potential disaster site, and in many cases constitutes a viable operational strategy. (2004:32)

The bulk of vulnerability studies advances such an empowered notion of local knowledge. For Kathleen Tierney too, communities mostly already possess the capacities needed for an effective response, but all too often, 'powerful social forces will stand in the way of such improvement' (2014:7). In this perspective, the task of the aid worker becomes to listen to the locals and help them exercise their knowledge in the forums and avenues that benefit them. In marked opposition to the technocratic approach to disaster, in vulnerability studies, there is a strong concern about speaking for people without a mandate. Ben Wisner emphasises the practice of creating open spaces to listen to local peoples' concerns and engage in knowledge-sharing on an equal footing. Wisner maintains that the task of the vulnerability scholar is to give voice to the marginalised and to reveal the hidden, but systemic violence that keeps local communities in situations of poverty. For Wisner, vulnerability is 'the blockage, erosion or devaluation of local knowledge and coping practices, or – taken together – local capacity' (2004:189). He argues there is a need to set free the people's 'social capital' (ibid.) and to liberate the 'creativity of the masses' (ibid.) to enable an effective and ethical recovery process.

Also disaster scholar Piers Blaikie advocates the idea of disaster relief as the creation of a free and open space to listen to the locals and learn from local expertise. Whereas the aid worker formerly exercised their scientific authority to regain mastery over a situation, vulnerability studies restricts their role to that of a facilitator and collaborator in the production of hybrid forms of expertise that blend local, vernacular skills with more centralised resources. Similar to Wisner, Blaikie conceptualises vulnerability as a condition of blockage to the realisation of a community's natural, unimpeded flourishing. For Blaikie, Cannon, Davis and Wisner the vulnerability approach:

[. . .] requires a genuine listening to local people [. . .] and an awareness of how power relations can block the participation of the most vulnerable. Indeed, as Chambers (1983) puts it, one must 'put the last first'. Doing so opens up a channel of communication between the people and disaster aid workers that goes beyond 'consultation'. People are able to express their needs and work together with outsiders to overcome obstacles. (1994:214)

What is the epistemological background of this connection between a location and a distinct form of knowledge? Indeed, what is the deeper justification of this valorisation of the local that emerges as privileged with regard to knowledge production? With its deconstruction of the authoritarian position of the knowing 'expert' and the reversal of the power hierarchy that now 'puts the last first', the epistemology advanced by the vulnerability approach emerged from within feminist and deconstructionist critiques of scientific objectivity, put forward in the 1970s. Let us take a deeper, historical look at 'local knowledge' before evaluating its effects when applied to Occupy Sandy.

LOCAL KNOWLEDGE AS SITUATED KNOWLEDGE

Arguing that established social-scientific paradigms presupposed the universality of a subject that was reality coded as white, male and heterosexual, deconstructionist and feminist social theory in the 1970s set out to challenge this bias by elaborating a 'successor science' that – rather than claiming universal knowledge – would be made up of several composite knowledges that did not deny their boundedness but were instead 'place-specific', 'local' or 'situated'. Along with Clifford Geertz' anthropological treatise *Local Knowledge* (1983),[37] Donna Haraway's essay *Situated Knowledges* (1988) can be seen to form the epistemic backbone of vulnerability studies' emphasis on local knowledge.

'Location is about vulnerability' (1991:196), wrote Donna Haraway in her book *Simians, Cyborgs and Women. The Reinvention of Nature.* In her work, Haraway develops a radically partial form of local knowledge she calls 'situated knowledge'. Her starting point is the radical multiplicity of a wide array of knowledges that are all incommensurable with one another. Having been formulated from particular standpoints, they do not share the same outlook, perspectives or concerns. For Haraway, every epistemology is situated and necessarily bounded by that situation. However, this does not mean giving up on the promise of objective knowledge, it just means that no viewpoint in itself is sufficient to provide the kind of panoramic overview traditionally associated with 'objectivity'. For Haraway, a situated objectivity can only be achieved through a democratic conversation between the partial positions; by creating a 'network of connections' (Haraway 1988:580) between standpoints, translating between 'power-differentiated-communities' (ibid.) and constructing a mediated subject position that is based on radical insufficiency and multiplicity. While Haraway does not argue that this objectivity is achieved in a power-free or neutral space, she has a lot of hope for situated knowledge as a 'wonderfully detailed, active, partial way of organising worlds' (ibid.:583), in which 'only partial perspective promises objectivity' (ibid.)

Like the vulnerability approach, Haraway advances a strong concept of 'partiality' to arrive at a more accurate and just epistemology. And like in Piers Blaikie's account of those vulnerable communities that came 'last' and now deserve to be put 'first', Haraway also believes in the epistemic advantage of the marginalised that now emerge as favoured among the array of partial knowledges. She frames her account of situated knowledge as emerging explicitly from the vulnerable position of marginality she calls the 'subjugated':

> Many currents in feminism attempt to theorise grounds for trusting especially the vantage points of the subjugated; there is good reason to believe vision is better from below the brilliant space platforms of the powerful. Building on that suspicion, this essay is an argument for situated and embodied knowledges [. . .] Subjugated standpoints are preferred because they seem to promise more adequate, sustained, objective, transforming accounts of the world. (ibid.:583–4)

At the outset of her essay, Haraway contrasts the position of the subjugated with the position of dominant mastery. For her, the essential difference is that 'we are the embodied others, who are not allowed not to have a body' (ibid.:575). Echoing a classical tenet in second wave feminism, the male, rational subject can imagine himself as disembodied, universal and capable of abstract thought, while the female is framed as an essentially corporeal creature, tied to bodily rhythms and incapable of rational inquiry. For Haraway, the essence of conventional social science lies in a stifling reduction of the object of study to an inert body that can be appropriated at will by the male knowledge-seeker. By being thus reduced to a mere 'object-for-knowledge', the object of study is denied any kind of agency or any potential for 'conversation' with the subject.

Haraway highlights how situated knowledge differs from the objectifying paradigm by creating a dialogical space that allows the object of study to speak back. For Haraway, the methodologies championed by the vulnerability approach (such as ethnography and participant observation) are exemplary 'critical approaches [. . .] where the agency of people studied itself transforms the entire project of producing social theory' (ibid.:592). Haraway calls this dialogue that does not disavow power differentials but instead attempts to productively overcome them as a new dialectic. While the Hegelian dialectic established the conditions for a productive encounter between subject and object in a scientific setting, for Haraway, it too quickly aborted this dialogue by sublating the encounter into a synthesis or a new fixed form. According to Haraway, what is needed instead is an open-ended dialectic between situated knowledges that together produce situated objectivity in a 'power-sensitive conversation' (ibid.:590). Haraway argues that this dialogue would truly dissolve the boundary between subject and object in the social sciences: 'Situated knowledges require that the object of knowledge be pictured as an actor and agent, not as a screen or a ground or a resource, never finally as slave to the master that closes off the dialectic in his unique agency and his authorship of "objective knowledge"' (ibid.:592).

Her references to the dialectic make Haraway's elaboration of situated knowledge a peculiar one that hovers uncomfortably between materialist and postmodern epistemologies. Certainly, the idea of an epistemic privilege, pertaining to those who are marginalised by power structures is common critical currency since Marx posited the proletariat as the epistemically privileged historical actor.[38] However, while Marxism, and later Marxist feminism, grounded this epistemic privilege in the centrality of 'the subjugated' to the capitalist mode of production and reproduction, whose negation gives 'the subjugated' their particular epistemic advantage, Haraway falls short of grounding 'situated knowledge' in anything outside the positioning of a subject *as* a marginal body. While she nuances her claim for 'situated knowledge' by asserting that 'to see from below is neither easily learned nor unproblematic, even if "we" "naturally" inhabit the great underground terrain of subjugated knowledges' (ibid.:584) she nevertheless seems to justify the existence of epistemic privilege simply *qua* natural inhabiting, rather than dialectically as the negative pole of a social totality.

Even so, vulnerability studies appears as a great leap forward, compared to the cold war command-and-control style of the Red Cross or FEMA. Since the 1970s, disaster scholars have flaunted the creation of a dialogical and open space, in which aid workers and disaster victims can exchange knowledge on how to best mitigate calamities. However, by neglecting the neoliberal reforms that accompanied the 1970s, this progressive image is keenly lacking an economic dimension. Let us return to Occupy Sandy to evaluate the applications of vulnerability studies to the current era.

THE STRANGE VICTORY OF OCCUPY SANDY

Occupy Sandy's overwhelming success practically confirms disaster studies' affirmation of local knowledge. But to what avail? In the autumn of 2013, one year after Superstorm Sandy, the Department of Homeland Security – the governmental body, founded by the Bush administration in response to the attacks on the World Trade Center, to combat terrorism and quell social dissent[39] – published a comprehensive report, endorsing the social movement's relief effort. Mirroring current disaster research (Dynes, 1994, Neal and Phillips 1995) the bulletin, *The Resilient Social Network* praised the efficacy of self-organised disaster relief, admitting the 'limitations of traditional relief efforts' (Ambinder, Jennings et al. 2013:3) to provide adequate aid services in an age of heightened disaster risk. In its 'Executive Summary' of the events, Homeland Security is unambiguous in its admiration for the social movement's relief effort:

> Within hours of Sandy's landfall, members from the Occupy Wall Street movement – a planned social movement comprised of social activists who protested income inequality in the United States – used social media to tap the wider Occupy network for volunteers and aid. Overnight, a volunteer army of young, educated, tech-savvy individuals with time and a desire to help others emerged. In the days, weeks, and months that followed, 'Occupy Sandy' became one of the leading humanitarian groups providing relief to survivors across New York City and New Jersey. At its peak, it had grown to an estimated 60,000 volunteers – more than four times the number deployed by the American Red Cross. (ibid.:1)

The Homeland Security report goes on to praise the relief effort in much the same vocabulary that we have seen vulnerability scholars adopt vis-à-vis local capacities. Enumerating five 'Occupy Sandy Success Drivers' that include 'the horizontal structure of Occupy Sandy' (ibid.:3), 'social media as the primary means to attract and mobilize a large volunteer corps' (ibid.), as well as, ironically, the 'Occupy Wall Street infrastructure' (ibid.), the stated purpose of the Homeland Security report is to 'determine how FEMA can coordinate response activities and capabilities with grassroots entities operating at the local level' (ibid.). Aiming to learn from Occupy Sandy's bottom-up approach, the report admiringly concludes that: 'unlike traditional disaster response organizations, there were no appointed leaders, no bureaucracy, no regulations to follow, no pre-defined mission, charter, or strategic plan. There was just relief' (ibid.:1).

How can we make sense of the strange proximity between the US government and Occupy Sandy? Wasn't Occupy Wall Street a resolutely anti-state social movement that protested against the governmental bailout of banks? Had the NYPD not attacked Occupiers with pepper spray and violently removed protesters from Zuccotti Park in the autumn of 2011? Just one year and one hurricane later, everything seemed different. Mayor Bloomberg went out to Brooklyn to pay tribute to the activists (Jaffe, 2012: para. 3). A few weeks later, Occupy was meeting with the NYPD and the National Guard to soak up their praise and coordinate contingency plans (Robbins, 2012: para. 1). After another few months, the social movement that had blockaded banks on Wall Street was filling out applications for government grants and soliciting donations for reconstruction from *Home Depot* (Maslin, 2013: para. 5).[40] What had happened?

A possible answer emerged when the Obama administration presented its budget for the fiscal year 2013. Quoting the 'superiority' of community-run disaster aid, the proposal suggested a $1 billion cut to FEMA's annual budget, amounting to a 14% budget reduction compared to the fiscal year 2012 (Khimm, 2012: para. 8, Homeland Security 2013:3).[41] As evidence indicated that self-help initiatives were more successful than government aid, disaster relief could be proposed as a prime area for reductions in government spending. This continued a trend begun by the Bush government that had significantly decimated FEMA funding by subsuming it under the Department of Homeland Security. As the eco-critical writer Rosemary Radford Ruether points out, FEMA was already 'greatly eroded under the Bush administration by funding cuts [. . .] where most of the funding went to anti-terror plans' (2006:179).

The policy of offsetting government deficits through cuts to social spending is known as austerity. Its application in the US can be traced back to the 1970s, when the post-war Keynesian productivity deal, in which high wages alongside generous social spending guaranteed a high level of welfare, entered a state of crisis. In competition with the economies of Japan and West Germany, the US productive power reached a limit, as markets gradually became saturated (Brenner, 2006). To overcome the economic downturn, the US government attempted to relaunch production through deindustrialisation. Heavy industry was moved offshore, in particular to Asia, where wages were lower. At the same time as the economy was being deindustrialised, the finance, insurance and real estate sectors received massive investments and favourable conditions in the form of deregulated markets and tax breaks in order to rekindle the economy through the financialisation of assets (Harvey 2005; McNally 2009).[42]

While production was deindustrialised, the primary way in which governments reduced federal overheads was by rolling back social spending on a massive scale. The political theorist Mikkel Bolt Rasmussen has described the era since the 1970s as 'one long crash landing [in which] capitalism has tried to reconstruct itself by saving on social reproduction through debt, technological development and the outsourcing of production' (2015:147). The dominant form this cutback takes is a drastic reduction in real wages, as well as in the social reproductive services of health care, education and emergency aid. For the average American, this had dire consequences, as Bolt Rasmussen confirms:

In the US the standard of living has dropped between 20 and 30% since the beginning of the 1970s and it is no longer possible to support a family with one paycheck (in the 1960s a working week of forty hours was enough to support a family, today 80 hours is often not enough), wage differences have exploded (since the 1970s the difference between the richest fifth of the US population and the poorest increased exponentially and is today bigger than in 1929). (ibid.:29)

With the state thus reduced to its core functions of security and market-pandering, disaster victims are left to their own devices, with grassroots organising and self-help initiatives often the only available options during calamity. While disaster studies embellishes scarcity through romantic references to local capacity and subjugated knowledge, self-help is simply what communities are left with under austerity. Referring to Naomi Klein's work on *Disaster Capitalism* (2007), the collective *Out of the Woods* has recently described the effects of austerity on the disaster sector. In the wake of massive reductions in governmental spending, communities are first exposed to disaster by development aggression, urban immiseration and the privatisation of infrastructure. Once the hurricane hits, disaster victims are made to pay for the reconstruction process out of their own, bloodied pockets:

> Since self-organised disaster communities are more effective than state agencies and market forces at responding to disasters, the state can simply sit back and let people suffer, then reassert itself when the community dissipates as normality returns. This is the state's interest in 'resilience', exposing proletarians to disaster, abandoning them to survive by their own efforts, and then moving in with the 'disaster capitalism' of reconstruction and gentrification once the moment of disaster has passed. (2014: para. 8)

We are now able to draw preliminary conclusions about the economic role of local knowledge in an era of austerity. While theories that championed grassroots organising may have had critical thrust in the 1970s, they have been outpaced by the real historical development of capitalism that culminates in the austerity state. Countering the technocratic disaster relief that followed WWII, scientific research, as well as the activist scene promoted the people's ability to survive alone and without the state. Unbeknownst to its actors and participants, however, this discourse emerged in parallel to the large-scale dismantling of federal welfare, in which the state withdrew from the task of maintaining its population alive and in good health. Rather than providing essential services like health care, pensions and disaster relief, these domains have been increasingly privatised, which has opened new and lucrative business avenues for capital (Harvey 2005; Adams 2012; Adams 2013). In a context where communities effectively have no other choice than to self-organise in order to remain alive, the possibility of the subjugated to 'speak back' and engage in a shared space of knowledge production is harnessed by institutions like Homeland Security and fed back into their systems of regulation and control. Citizen initiatives have thus unwittingly legitimised neoliberal reforms towards the privatization of aid. By claiming a deliberately 'insufficient', 'partial', and 'multiple' perspective, vulnerability studies neglects the role of local knowledge in the reproduction of the very vulnerable conditions it set out to fight. The time is thus ripe for a paradigm shift.

I suggest that what is needed for disaster studies to again become critical is a different relation to vulnerability. We have seen that the prevailing relation that scholars and activists adopt towards the vulnerable is an endorsement of their local knowledge, whose particular capacities are championed in the fight against disaster. However, a closer look at the aftermath of Superstorm Sandy has shown that this valorisation has today become problematic. Intended to build autonomy and self-determination vis-à-vis the state, the affirmation of local knowledge becomes counterproductive, once the self-sufficiency of communities becomes a mandated state policy. When citizens were made to 'shoulder the burden of the failed state' (Kilkenny, 2013: para. 3), Occupy Sandy quickly became a necessary communitarian engagement under conditions of scarcity. With this, however, it also lost its unique value as an oppositional practice.

In a different critical register, and as cultural theorist McKenzie Wark has recently remarked, the position of the vulnerable has for decades been called 'the labor point of view' (Wark, 2015:28). Applying this materialist viewpoint to Occupy Sandy, we find a different relation to vulnerability that, instead of championing resilience to survive our capitalist present, criticises the function of vulnerability between the state, the market and community. Let us explore this possibility before concluding.

DISASTERS FROM THE LABOUR POINT OF VIEW

What can the labour point of view tell us today? Does it not hark back to a bygone era? To state socialism and the dream of a society modelled on the collective worker? On the contrary, for the cultural theorist Michael Denning the need for a labour viewpoint emerges precisely in response to the crisis that beset the left, following the West's large-scale deindustrialisation that transformed formerly industrial societies into consumer economies. This shift meant that long-rehearsed Marxist patterns of explanation, based on the gradual victory of the proletariat, became increasingly untenable, as the post-war *New Left* struggled to develop critical accounts of post-industrial society and its declining proletarian identity. In Denning's words, the central question was:

How to invent a Marxism without class. How could one maintain the insights and political drive of historical materialism in an epoch where left, right and center generally agreed that the classes of Fordist capitalism were passing from the stage of world history, when the 'labour metaphysic' [. . .] seemed irrelevant. (2004:84)[43]

For Denning, the *New Left* responded to the changes in the world economy by developing two dominant theoretical models. The first centred on the market and commodity culture as the structuring determinants of capitalist life. The second focused on the state and its fine-tuned modes of government. Denning equates the market-based model with the analyses of Guy Debord and the state-based model with the figure of Michel Foucault. However, Denning notes that in both accounts, work is conspicuously absent. It is here that the demand for a labour viewpoint arises. Reviewing the humanities landscape since the 1960s, Denning describes 'our reluctance to represent work' (2004:91) and the fact that in most social-scientific accounts 'work remains invisible' (ibid.:92). How can we apply the labour viewpoint to disasters and what can its application teach us today?

I have argued throughout that we ought to see different forms of social action as labour, meaning as productive or reproductive activity under capitalism. Through the wage, capitalism socially validates some activities – such as work in factories, state-infrastructures and offices – as labour, while framing other activities as unworthy of pay. We have seen that the reproduction of capitalism necessitates the interplay between two distinct spheres; a commercial sector where activities are performed for a direct market profit, and a non-commercial sector where activities are performed at a remove from immediate market interest.[44] Borrowing from the social reproduction theorists Maya Gonzales and Jeanne Neton, we have called the first sector the directly market mediated sphere (DMM), and the second sector the indirectly market mediated sphere (IMM) that together constitute the totality of capitalist productive and reproductive relations (Gonzales and Neton, 2014:153).

While corporations occupy the DMM sphere, the state has historically occupied the IMM sphere, in which civil servants provided health care, education, public infrastructure and disaster relief as social services, free of charge.[45] Formerly firmly in the sphere of state-led social reproduction, since the crisis of the 1970s, states have been increasingly 'unwilling to organise IMM activities, since they are a mere cost' (Gonzales and

Neton, 2014:169). In the US, emergency budgets have been significantly cut, despite an increasing disaster-rate. Some of these services were privatised and transformed into commercial DMM activities in the form of insurances and private security services, constituting the classical operation of disaster capitalism (Klein 2007). What is ignored by theorists of disaster capitalism, however, is that more often than not commercial operators do not seem to find these operations profitable, since they are confronted with impoverished communities who cannot pay for the added security in their lives. As a consequence, in the majority of cases, relief work stays in the IMM sphere but becomes the unwaged responsibility of neighbours, victims and volunteers.

Faced with this crisis, activists of social movements such as Occupy – many of whose members were unemployed (Hintze, 2014: para. 16) – have begun organising essential community services by themselves.[46] However, despite Occupy's effort to provide 'solidarity' rather than 'charity', these activities are haunted by their complicity with the neoliberal transfer of social responsibility onto voluntary aid providers. In the worst case, social movements are in this way helping to create the austerity state. The labour viewpoint suggests the inability to affirm self-organisation when it plays into the neoliberal idea of the *Big Society*, in which members of the community perform formerly state-run services as unpaid labour.[47] This highlights a new political situation, in which disaster studies' classical opposition between the state and civil society appears as definitively superseded. How can we characterise this new configuration between society, the market and the state? Re-examining the notion of vulnerability that forms the cornerstone of self-organised relief practices can provide us with an answer to this question.

Writing on the neoliberal conjuncture since the 1970s, the anthropologist Didier Fassin highlights the particular role of vulnerability in the contemporary political landscape. Fassin asserts that vulnerability has today become a key concept, embodied in the practice of humanitarianism. For Fassin, '[humanitarianism] relates to [. . .] the treatment of the poor, immigrants, abused women, children affected by poverty – in short, all those categories constituted in terms of "vulnerability"' (2010:269). The perspective of vulnerability entails a general shift in political practice and activist rhetoric to a grammar of suffering, in which human life emerges as the ultimate civic good, in need of protection. Enhancing Denning's diagnostic of a market-based and a state-based analysis of the present, we can argue that humanitarianism represents the third pillar on which contemporary government rests:

> We could even say that philanthropic politics is a sort of moral counterpart to the contemporaneous development of both the police state, understood as the ensemble of apparatuses maintaining security and control of populations, and classical liberal reason, understood as the emergence of economic activity into the field of power [. . .] Under this hypothesis, modern governance would rest not on two but on three pillars: to the police and liberalism, we should thus add humanitarianism. (Fassin, 2010:272)

Fassin emphasises that in contrast to state agents, the quintessential humanitarian actors are members of civil society and non-governmental organisations. He further specifies that as a consequence of its non-parliamentarianism, humanitarianism draws its vital force precisely from its apparent opposition to the state. While humanitarian organisations see themselves as firmly 'on the side of life' (ibid.:276), Fassin argues 'they have to place political actors on the side of death' (ibid.), resulting in an ostensible opposition to the state.[48] Counter to this self-proclaimed opposition, Fassin outlines the contemporary embedding of humanitarian practices at the very heart of a new governmental rationale that spans the state, the market and civil society and that he calls *Humanitarian Reason* (2012).

The case of Occupy Sandy serves as a counter-history to the way in which community-run disaster aid presents itself today. Rather than in opposition to the state, self-organised social reproduction integrates itself functionally into a new interplay between the state, the market and civil society that constitutes the heart of 'Humanitarian Reason'. By proving that the people can survive alone and by themselves, it alleviates the charges against state-administered austerity by maintaining social reproduction in conditions of scarcity.

Faced with this dilemma, what does our disaster landscape look like? For the Department of Homeland Security, it looks like this: 'If there will be more disasters in the future, and there will be, then there will be more opportunities, opportunities like Occupy Sandy' (Ambinder, Jennings et al., 2013:21). From the labour point of view, we can say that *becoming opportunities* is what has to be resisted. Instead, social movements providing disaster aid will have to enter into real conflict with existing capitalist relations. They will have to consider their role within the wider frame of social reproduction and invent new strategies – from leveraging demands to going on strike – since a movement that merely performs *relief labour* for free does not break with communities' state-imposed vulnerability. It might achieve improvements and incremental ameliorations, but it will not put an end to the political structures that expose populations to disaster across the globe.

8

The Separated Society

In this society unity appears as accidental, separation as normal.

— Karl Marx

In her ethnographic study of long-term disaster recovery in New Orleans, Vincanne Adams (2013) tells the story of Gerald. Displaced by Hurricane Katrina, Gerald returned home after three months in exile to find his house destroyed and uninhabitable. Living off social security, but with no mailing address, Gerald was unsure where his benefit cheques were sent. Wanting to access his meagre savings, he went to his bank but discovered that his branch had been flooded. Not qualifying for any of the FEMA emergency shelters because he was accompanied by his pet dog, Gerald slept in his car, trying to figure out what to do next. One day, with his cash savings dwindling and on the verge of destitution, he was picked up by a group of Canadian volunteers from the Good News Camp, a Christian faith-based aid organisation that set up shop in New Orleans only days after the hurricane hit the city. By the time they met Gerald, the volunteers managed a temporary shelter, medical facilities and a soup kitchen. At its peak, the organisation hosted over 17,000 volunteers from across North America.

Good News Camp was no isolated case. New Orleans saw a huge outpour of public and private sympathy in the wake of Hurricane Katrina. It is estimated that by 2009, as many as 1.5 million volunteers came to the region to assist the reconstruction process, founding over 500 new charities, not all of them faith-based (Adams, 2013:133). Among the most well-known is the Common Ground Relief Collective, founded by the former Black Panther member Malik Rahim. Under the slogan 'Solidarity not Charity', Common Ground ran community programmes such as a health clinic, legal counselling services, as well as home-construction assistance, gutting houses and doing repair work. Regardless of whether their motivations were secular or religious, the volunteer groups in New Orleans shared one and the same goal: to step in where the federal government had fallen short. Vincanne Adams sums up the paradox of this gesture at a time when the federal government systematically withdrew from providing adequate disaster relief:

> The large response of charities, nongovernmental grass-roots, and faith-based organizations was overwhelming in the case of post-Katrina New Orleans. It was also both a critique of the failure of federal subcontracting companies – the inefficient work of FEMA, Road Home, the Small Business Administration (SBA), and insurance companies – and an endorsement of the neoliberal policies that set these failed programs in motion. The fact is, the federal government had for some years been calling on the charity sector to do just this, to fill in where their own programs had failed. (Adams, 2013:127–8)[49]

Organisations such as Good News Camp and Common Ground Collective challenge us to rethink the role of community-run disaster relief in times of austerity. What is the value of self-organised social reproduction when its provision runs the risk of justifying the state's austerity measures? The history of disaster aid during the Short American Century leaves us with many such paradoxes that demand a thorough theorisation of the changing economic relation between the state and civil society in the last half of the twentieth century. The foregoing case studies marked out the entwined trajectory of these two spheres through their involvement in the reproductive labour of disaster relief. I zoomed in on two moments of crisis, in which the changing relation between these social spheres is made manifest. First, the Great Depression of the 1930s, in which disaster aid became a federal responsibility under a strong, social-democratic state. Second, the deindustrialisation of the 1970s, in which the federal state gradually withdrew from the provision of aid services, shifting the responsibility for relief back onto civil society. On one side, we have the New Deal and Keynesianism; on the other, neoliberalism and austerity. We can view both state responses as adequate to their economic conditions of emergence, while subsuming them under a vaster historical narrative of crisis. Let us recapitulate the characteristics of these two historical moments before evaluating the relation between state and civil society during disasters today.

With the New Deal, the ensuing war economy and the post WWII reconstruction, the Great Depression could be momentarily overcome through ample federal investments into the welfare of workers, which spurred buying power and reinvigorated the economy. Disaster-prone states such as Florida and California received generous cash injections to rebuild their infrastructure, employing thousands and extending real estate development to previously inaccessible regions. As early as the 1960s, however, the productive power of the US began to wane again. This time, the response was austerity, rather than federal largesse. Replacing Keynesianism with Chicago School neoliberalism, the government began cutting social spending to limit the growing domestic debt. For the disaster sector, this meant that relief moved from being the purview of the federal government to being the communitarian responsibility that it had been until the late nineteenth century.

Within this shift from the state-funded disaster aid of the New Deal to the withdrawal of the state from the reproductive labour of relief, the Black Panther Party's self-organised welfare programmes form a telling hinge at the tail-end of the extension of state-led social reproduction. Recognising the untruthfulness of the state's and capital's promises of full employment and permanent upward mobility, the Panthers tried to strengthen their community by providing self-organised medical, nutritional and educational services. However, while the Black Panthers were successful in self-organising social reproduction, even forcing the state to further extend its welfare portfolio to marginalised populations, their actions at the same time presaged the new responsibility that befalls civil society in the age of austerity. When, starting in the 1970s, the state gradually withdrew from the provision of welfare services, communities had no other choice but to shoulder the reproductive burden themselves. From this moment on, self-organised social reproduction has run the risk of legitimising the state's austerity regime by proving that the people can survive alone and without state assistance. For Vincanne Adams, this paradox constitutes the major contradiction regarding self-organisation during disasters:

> The recent rise in the number of nonprofit, non-governmental organizations, service groups, and humanitarian and charity-based aid organizations in the United States now [. . .] must be seen at least in part as a direct outcome of policy commitments to the basic philosophical assumption that the government *should not* be responsible

for taking care of its needy citizens when the private sector can and should do this job better. (Adams, 2013:128)

THE INTEGRATION OF SELF-ORGANISATION

While on the rise in the 1970s, the Black Panthers' form of radical self-organisation almost completely disappeared in the 1980s and 1990s. Instead, grassroots community organising became absorbed into the neoliberal policy shift from state-led to community-led social reproduction. This shift saw a strong valorisation of aspirational community work as a means to escape poverty. It is visible in the Clinton era policy reforms that provided the backdrop to the Chicago Heat Wave. Attempting to tackle the phenomenon of inner-city poverty, Clinton's policymakers claimed that the roots of material destitution were to be found not in external conditions of inequality, but within poor communities themselves. According to the African American sociologist William Julius Wilson, President Clinton's right hand man in tackling inner city poverty, the culprit was 'welfare dependency', which allegedly maintained poor black communities in inherited destitution, passed on from generation to generation (Joseph, Chaskin et al., 2007:374).

Holding on to the promises of upward mobility and social integration that had been championed by the Civil Rights Movement, black community leaders and local politicians embraced an entrepreneurial do-it-yourself ethos that saw access to high paying jobs as the key to increasing social respectability and wealth. Often this took the form of social activists forming alliances with politicians, business leaders or real estate developers. In his study of housing reform in New Orleans, sociologist John Arena details how:

> The St. Thomas community and their activist allies forged a partnership with [. . .] the city's most powerful real estate developer, to privatize the development and create a new 'mixed-income' community that would drastically reduce the number of affordable apartments. From protesting federal and local government initiatives to scale [sic] back public housing, tenant leaders and advisers moved to embrace the Clinton administration's [. . .] HOPE VI federal grant, designed to privatize and downsize public housing. (Arena, 2012:xviii)

In the 1980s and 1990s, activists and community leaders for the most part underwrote the shift away from state-led social reproduction and embraced the 'vitality of the market' (Cisneros and Engdahl, 2009:11) to combat poverty. This willingness to participate in governmental reform was complimented by an active inclusion of local activists by the political and financial elite. Looking back at the Clinton years, the former Secretary of Housing and Urban Development (HUD), Henry Cisneros, has underlined the importance of integrating the non-profit sector and important interest groups from the 1960s and 1970s to tackle key social issues in an un-bureaucratic way (ibid.:12). This inclusion would be unproblematic if it actually benefitted poor African American communities. Instead, it only benefitted a fraction of that community for a limited amount of time. Instead of rising social integration and wealth, the 1980s saw a drastic increase in black unemployment, resulting in skyrocketing poverty, a trend that has continued unabated into the twenty-first century. According to statistics from the Pew Research Center, between 2005 and 2009, the average black household wealth fell by more than 50%, while white household wealth 'only' fell by 16% (2011: para. 3).

Faced with this profound reproductive crisis, the integration of community organisations into political decision-making confronts us with a dilemma: On the one hand, community activists have more chances than ever to have their voices heard and to influence political decision-making. Since the 1980s, a plethora of programmes have been put in place that enable the exchange between community organisers and government officials. On the other hand, we'd do well to see these schemes essentially as an outcome of austerity. Since deindustrialisation, the federal state has attempted to reduce the costs of social spending wherever it can. This has severely affected the FEMA disaster relief budget, which the Obama administration cut by a total of $582 million between 2016 and 2017 (Office of Management and Budget, 2017:110). The inclusion of actors from civil society is thus a necessary means for the government to maintain key social services, while saving on federal expenses.

However, since the 2008 financial crisis, there has been a renaissance of resistant attempts to self-organise disaster aid against capital and the austerity state. In this domain, Occupy Sandy constitutes the most sophisticated and large-scale recent undertaking. However, as the counter-intuitive endorsement of the social movement by the Department of Homeland Security shows, even an outspokenly leftist grassroots organisation such as Occupy risks playing into the hands of the government's austerity agenda. Against the good intentions of community organisers, in a situation like this, the economy takes precedence over ideology, since the political prestige that Occupy gained by helping citizens in need is trumped by the government's budgetary calculations that rely on civil society efforts to maintain their legitimacy. When entrepreneurial bottom-up organising becomes a mandated state policy for running everything from health care provision to disaster relief, the resistant energies that can be mobilised by civil society have to be critically rethought. The question then becomes: How to self-organise disaster aid (and other reproductive services) in a way that resists being co-opted by the neoliberal reforms of the state?

THE NEGATIVITY OF LABOUR

In contrast to industrial labour politics, where solidarity was achieved through a shared experience of work, reproductive labour does not immediately offer the same possibilities for unification. While industrial workers came together in the factory and could unite, based on a shared experience of deskilled labour, in the reproductive sector, jobs mostly retain their singular skillset. During disasters, we are faced with the increasing atomisation of different groups and individuals with vastly different objectives; salaried civil servants working for the state, NGO foot soldiers in search of the next big donor, informally organised volunteers, dispersed activists and digital humanitarians. None of these actors share the same mission, interest or motivation. On the ground, they confront each other as competitors for limited resources. While cooperation and association do happen in every disaster situation, it is difficult to envision the kind of solidarity that could give rise to a unified structure, able to challenge the state's austerity measures. With reproductive labour, the socialist ideal of the collective worker inevitably breaks down.

If they are not united through a shared horizon of work, how can community-run relief organisations develop labour solidarity? Rather than in the positive experience of 'being in it together', I want to suggest that disaster solidarity might instead be found negatively, in the adverse experience of being abandoned by the state and by capital. Over and over, capital and the state expose the inhabitants of disaster-prone regions to the dangers of natural and social emergencies. Over and over, disaster victims are left alone in situations of need, just to be made responsible for their own recovery. Abandoned by the state, they are also abandoned by capital, since they do not possess the economic resources of value to disaster capitalists. In the context of such a double abandonment, we should see disaster aid soberly as what it is; a reproductive service that the state has become loath to do.

Viewing disaster relief not as a communitarian responsibility, but as the management of what has been left behind by capital and the state enables political strategies that are foreclosed by the fuzzy romanticism of community organising. It allows us to formulate demands on the basis of managing those domains of social reproduction that the state has abandoned, while also opening up to strike and refusal as viable political strategies. Though certainly no recipe for a post-capitalist future, seeing disaster relief as reproductive labour guards us against naively embracing the sentimentalism of resilience, with its readymade dogmas, political fads, and past shibboleths about coming together in times of crisis. Instead, this negative position allows us to see disasters as something imposed on us from the outside; by the neglect of capitalism and the state that offer us no positive point of identification. When in the current catastrophic conjuncture, social reproduction becomes a major terrain of class struggle, we have to invent forms of organising that are adequate to this new battleground. In this calamitous arena, disasters are a place to start.

9

2020: I Can't Breathe

At the time of writing, the world is in the stranglehold of the most wide-reaching disaster in recent history. Following the mutation of a new Coronavirus strain in Wuhan, China in December 2019, and its rapid spread through Asia and Europe, the United States have now become the epicentre of the outbreak. The novel Coronavirus, or SARS-CoV-2, is the pathogen responsible for the acute respiratory illness of Covid-19. Erratic in its effects, the disease remains asymptomatic for some, while others experience high fevers, dry coughs and shortness of breath. Though the exact causes that lead to a lethal outcome remain unknown, in the worst cases, the infection causes patients to slowly suffocate, their lungs filling with fluid first, then eventually rupturing. This process is often accompanied by multi-organ failure, blood clots, septic shock and cytokine storm syndrome, in which the immune system turns against itself and attacks the body. Impossible as it is to verify the exact number of Coronavirus deaths, the Johns Hopkins University Coronavirus Research Center estimates that as of 20 July 2020, Covid-19 has killed 606,206 people worldwide, over a fifth of which in the United States.[50]

Though public health experts had, over the last years, repeatedly warned of the dangers of an imminent global pandemic, the USA was shockingly ill-prepared for the outbreak. In January 2019, the US Intelligence Community published its *Worldwide Threat Assessment*, an evaluation of the relative gravity of a series of possible incumbent hazards, including cyber-operations, terrorism, counterintelligence and organised crime. Regarding global health, the consortium wrote that

the United States and the world will remain vulnerable to the next flu pandemic or large-scale outbreak of a contagious disease that could lead to massive rates of death and disability, severely affect the world economy, strain international resources, and increase calls on the United States for support [. . .] The growing proximity of humans and animals has increased the risk of disease transmission. The number of outbreaks has increased in part because pathogens originally found in animals have spread to human populations. (Coats, 2019:21)

In line with this worrying assessment, in September 2019, the Johns Hopkins Center for Health Security issued a report titled, *Preparedness for a High-Impact Respiratory Pathogen Pandemic*, with the following predictions:

> Were a high-impact respiratory pathogen to emerge [. . .] it would likely have significant public health, economic, social, and political consequences [. . .] The combined possibilities of short incubation periods and asymptomatic spread can result in very small windows for interrupting transmission, making such an outbreak difficult to contain. (Nuzzo, Mullen, Snyder et al., 2019:6)

Although the alarm bells had been rung by the highest-ranking American public health officials, predicting the current outbreak down to the smallest details – including animal-to-human transmission and the dangers of asymptomatic spreaders – nothing was done to prepare. Instead, when the first cases of Covid-19 began to surface in New York City in early March 2020, Mayor Bill de Blasio encouraged New Yorkers to 'go on with [their] lives + get out on the town despite Coronavirus' (Graff, 2020: para. 1), while Health Commissioner Oxiris Barbot surmised that 'there's no indication that being in a car, being in the subways with someone who's potentially sick is a risk factor' (cited in Edelman, 2020: para. 13). Only three weeks later, the New York City case count had increased to over 5,000, forcing the Mayor's Office to review its nonchalance. On 22 March, New York's governor Andrew Cuomo issued an executive order instituting shelter in place restrictions, effectively placing New York City under lockdown. Regrettably, this measure came too late. At the time of writing, the USA tops the worldwide list of certified Coronavirus infections at 3,773,260, with 140,534 reported deaths. New York is by far the most severely affected state, with infection numbers totalling at 434,164 and deaths at 32,570 – not far off those of the whole of Italy.

In contrast to the more localised calamities discussed throughout, this time, the role of disaster as the harbinger of a crisis in social reproduction was glaringly obvious. In a gigantic transvaluation of values occurring almost overnight, productive labour was halted and the reproductive labour taking place in hospitals, care facilities and households moved to the forefront of public attention. At the same time, the outbreak revealed the staggering funding shortages within the state-led social-reproductive sphere, in which everything – from personal protective equipment (PPE) to ventilators to medical staff – was in short supply (Schlanger, 2020: para. 1). Harrowing reports from the clinical frontlines revealed that almost 40 per cent of American hospitals had no remaining face shields (ibid.: para. 6); whilst 34 per cent had no thermometers and almost 20 per cent had run out of medical gowns (ibid.). In mid-March, as the pandemic gathered speed, the *New York Times* reported that the first health centres were considering shutting down for lack of medical equipment, while in others, doctors were intubating Coronavirus patients with simple surgical masks, rather than with antiviral respirator masks (Jacobs, Richtel & Baker, 2020: para. 1), endangering not only their own lives but that of their patients, friends and families.

As infection numbers climbed exponentially throughout March and April, more and more doctors and nurses fell ill, creating an acute staff shortage in hospitals nationwide. Counterintuitively, the lack of care personnel did not lead to a spike in hiring. Instead, cash-strapped clinics struggled to make do by gearing their entire service provision towards the treatment of Covid-19 patients, halting everything from non-essential operations to cancer treatments and retraining anybody from anaesthetists to oncology nurses as ad-hoc intensive care staff for Coronavirus patients (Cleeland, 2020: para. 3). As an emergency doctor in Manhasset, New York put it:

We are now a monolith. We started with a medical ICU, surgical ICU, cardiac ICU, neurosurgical ICU, and a cardiothoracic ICU, plus a dozen mixed specialty floors. Every floor and unit is becoming a COVID unit. There is no more specialization – we're all treating one thing. (cited in ibid.: para. 4)

Despite this herculean effort, the New York medical system was soon overwhelmed. At some clinics, over 200 doctors and nurses contracted Covid-19, but were required to keep on working, regardless of their symptoms (Schwirtz, 2020, para. 4). Instead of requiring sick staff to self-isolate, Craig R. Smith, surgeon-in-chief at the New York Presbyterian Hospital, informed his overstretched personnel that: 'Our health care systems are at war with a pandemic virus [. . .] You are expected to keep fighting with whatever weapons you're capable of working [. . .] Sick is relative [. . .] That means you come to work. Period (cited in ibid.: para. 20).

But medical machismo has rarely stopped a virus. As more and more medical staff were withdrawn from service in severe respiratory distress, government officials did what they always do when state-led social reproduction falters: they drew on the voluntary sector to fill the gaps in their ailing service provision. Calls were issued to medical students, retired doctors and out-of-state nurses to join the relief effort in New York (Cleeland, 2020: para. 15). At the same time, countless mutual aid initiatives sprang up all over the country to counter the shortcomings of the floundering medical sector.[51] At the headquarters of St. Joseph Health in Providence, volunteers gathered with fabric, scissors and rubber bands to improvise face masks for thousands of care workers (Jacobs, Richtel & Baker, 2020: para. 33). Influencers used their social media reach to instruct Youtubers on how to cobble together face masks – no sewing needed. The *Minnesota COVIDSitters*, a group of students from the University of Minnesota Medical School, organised grocery runs and childcare for thinly stretched hospital workers (Tolentino, 2020: para. 7). In Manhattan, the *Invisible Hands* group shopped essentials for immunocompromised residents who were unable to leave their houses (ibid: para. 5). Locally organised, these grassroots organisations used global media, such as WhatsApp groups and Google Docs, to create databases of residents in need and coordinate aid efforts in real time.

Writing in the *New Yorker*, journalist Jia Tolentino has chronicled the manifold mutual aid practices, from the mundane to the heavily politicised, that sprang up across the nation in the wake of Covid-19:

In Aurora, Colorado, a group of librarians started assembling kits of essentials for the elderly [. . .] Disabled people in the Bay Area organized assistance for one another; a large collective in Seattle set out explicitly to help 'Undocumented, LGBTQI, Black, Indigenous, People of Color, Elderly, and Disabled, folxs who are bearing the brunt of this social crisis.' Undergrads helped other undergrads who had been barred from dorms and cut off from meal plans. Prison abolitionists raised money so that incarcerated people could purchase commissary soap. And, in New York City [. . .] Relief funds were organized for movie-theatre employees, sex workers, and street vendors. (2020: para. 2)

While commenting on the long history of mutual aid as a radical practice, Tolentino notes that, with the outbreak of the Coronavirus, mutual aid 'entered the mainstream' (ibid: para. 30) and 'suddenly seemed to be everywhere,' (ibid: para. 3). Observing the generalised outpour of solidarity, she concludes that 'mutual aid [. . .] has entered the lexicon of the coronavirus era alongside "social distancing" and "flattening the curve"' (ibid.). The same jubilant tone was struck by other liberal media outlets, with the *New York Times* surmising that quarantine was 'the perfect time to get (virtually) close to your community' (Warzel, 2020: para.1) and encouraging readers to 'join a mutual aid network' (ibid.). Addressing a younger readership, *Teen Vogue* ran a long feature on mutual aid that grouped together under the same heading, the philanthropic actions of celebrities, such as rapper Lil Nas X and basketball player Zion Williamson, and the grassroots efforts of *NYC United Against Coronavirus*, which organised pickups of coffee, soap and disinfectant (Diavolo, 2020).

Alongside the liberal media, politicians too fell over themselves in praise of mutual aid. The Democrat Representative Alexandria Ocasio-Cortez extolled the virtues of community organising in a public conference call with the prison abolitionist Mariame Kaba:

> We can buy into the old frameworks of, when a disaster hits, it's every person for themselves. Or we can affirmatively choose a different path. And we can build a different world, even if it's just on our building floor, even if it's just in our neighborhood, even if it's just on our block. [We don't have to wait] for Congress to pass a bill, or the President to do something. (cited in Tolentino, 2020: para. 6)

Over the course of the preceding chapters, I have defined mutual aid – i.e. the practice in which community members pool their resources to help each other in times of need – as civil-society-led social reproduction. What can conceptualising the mutual aid initiatives responding to Covid-19 in the vocabulary of Marxist feminism contribute to our understanding of the current situation? Firstly, viewing mutual aid as self-organised social reproduction embeds community-run relief practices in the wider totality of reproductive labour. Indeed, from the perspective of social reproduction, the labour of maintaining individuals and communities alive has historically been shouldered by three distinct social spheres. It can be carried out as a non-profit activity by the state, which has developed sophisticated welfare services to optimise the labour-power of the population; or by market actors as a directly for-profit activity. In these first two cases, social reproductive labour is performed in exchange for a wage, making it a socially recognised form of work. However, as I have shown, most social reproductive labour remains unwaged. It is carried out daily and without remuneration by family members and community networks, invested in collective well-being. Disconnected from the state and the market – in an immediate sense at least – mutual aid falls in the latter category. It represents unpaid, indirectly market-mediated social reproduction and is therefore rarely recognised as work.

During the pandemic, the social-reproductive burden was unevenly split between all three spheres. With the state sector in retreat, responsibility for social reproduction was outsourced to the market and to civil society, completing the triangulation of social reproduction under austerity. While the Trump administration privatised Coronavirus testing by selling corporate licenses to the two big pharmaceutical companies Quest and LabCorp, (Hartmann, 2020: para. 1) instead of using the World Health Organization's affordable and readily available test kits, mutual aid initiatives attempted to remedy the state's shortcomings by filling the gaps in its service provision, providing unwaged reproductive labour to the community where the state and the market faltered.

Secondly, defining mutual aid during Covid-19 as civil-society-led social reproduction forces us to look at the practice in relation to other agents of social reproduction, particularly the state. Tolentino notes that 'historically, in the United States, mutual-aid networks have proliferated mostly in communities that the state has chosen not to help' (2020: para. 14). The foregoing case studies have similarly shown how self-organised practices emerged in the fissures of state-led social reproduction, filling the gaps in the state's service provision – often outspokenly in opposition to the state. While self-organised social reproduction was able to bring about critical change in the 1960s and 1970s, by drawing attention to the state's systematic neglect of parts of the political community and demanding inclusion into federal welfare, I have highlighted how the advent of austerity dealt a fatal blow to self-organised social reproduction. As the welfare state was increasingly dismantled in the 1980s, unpaid reproductive labour became the mandated policy of social service retrenchment. Under austerity, mutual aid risks legitimating governmental withdrawal by covering domains of social reproduction that the state has abandoned.

Mutual Aid during Covid-19 was no exception. When politicians such as Ocasio-Cortez call on civil society to step in where the state retreats, they are effectively absolving the government from amplifying its reproductive services. Seeing mutual aid during Covid-19 as the management of those reproductive domains that both the state and capital have left behind guards us against the easy romanticisation of community organising to which the liberal media and its politicians are so prone.

Thirdly, a social reproduction approach to the pandemic gives us a more nuanced picture of Covid-19 vulnerability than that offered by a narrowly medical view. Shortly after the Coronavirus outbreak, the US Center for Disease Control and Prevention (CDC) isolated a number of risk groups that were particularly susceptible to a severe progression of the illness. These included the immunocompromised, people with a history of heart conditions, sickle cell disease, chronic kidney disease, obesity and diabetes, asthma and hypertension (CDC, 2020: para. 1–2). By suggesting that Coronavirus vulnerability was determined by an individual's pre-existing health conditions, the public health data couched vulnerability to the virus in the singularity of medical history, making it into a personal, rather than political matter. In accordance with the data, people with pre-existing health conditions were asked to pay particular heed, to 'shield', and to adopt extra safety measures wherever they could.

Reports from the clinical frontlines, however, suggested a different picture: namely, that the intersection of race and class played a decisive role in both Covid-19 infection and mortality. Comparing mortality data across different states, an article in *MEDPAGE TODAY* revealed that:

> In Louisiana, African Americans accounted for 70% of COVID-19 deaths, while comprising 33% of the population. In Michigan, they accounted for 14% of the population and 40% of deaths, and in Chicago, 56% of deaths and 30% of the population. In New York, black people are twice as likely as white people to die from the coronavirus [. . .] Predominantly black US counties are experiencing a three-fold higher infection rate and a six-fold higher death rate than predominantly white counties. (Hlavinka, 2020: para. 3–6)

Shocked into action by this staggering death differential, a consortium of civil rights groups and doctors called on the US government to release Coronavirus-related data on race and ethnicity. Even though the CDC had long been cataloguing data on ethnicity, prior to the appeal, its public reports differentiated victims only according to sex, age and previous health conditions, omitting race as a crucial vulnerability factor. While from the CDC's viewpoint, race could appear as an incidental characteristic, thus hardly worth dwelling upon, a social reproduction perspective reveals race as a key determinant in the intergenerational transmission of health risks, in which black Americans experience a clear reproductive disadvantage. How does connecting Covid-19 vulnerability to communities' socio-economic conditions of production and reproduction change the CDC's account of individual risk factors? To begin, let us note that the CDC's primary vulnerability factors, hypertension and diabetes, are highly correlated with race: 'African Americans shoulder a higher burden of chronic disease, with 40% higher rates of hypertension and 60% higher rate of diabetes than white Americans, both of which have been tied to negative COVID-19 outcomes' (Hlavinka, 2020: para. 13).

Moreover, beyond the strictly medical realm, the disproportionate vulnerability of African Americans during the pandemic has been palpable in all areas of social life. In the workplace, it was evidenced by the fact that, in New York City, 75 per cent of 'frontline' workers in the care sector, public transport and the postal service are people of colour (ibid.: para. 9).[52] With self-isolation often impossible, many African Americans have continued to work throughout the pandemic, endangering their own lives and those of their families. Living conditions too confirm this trend. Indeed, according to data from the Economic Policy Institute, black families are 'more than twice as likely to live in densely populated housing structures as white households' (Gould and Wilson, 2020: fig. N), which makes virus transmission within the home almost unavoidable.

Economically, this vulnerability is legible in the disproportionate unemployment rates the pandemic has caused among black Americans. Between February and April 2020, African American unemployment rose to 16.7 per cent, compared to 12.2 per cent for white Americans (Gould and Wilson, 2020: fig. A). Although the US economy showed slow signs of recovery in May, the figures indicate that black workers are being left out. As white unemployment fell by two percentage points over the course of the month, black unemployment continued to rise unabatedly (Rattner and Higgins, 2020: para. 2). Dwindling job prospects in turn disproportionately affect black households, who on average dispose of only 18 per cent of the cash savings of white households (Gould and Wilson, 2020: fig. K). Moreover, while constituting a mere ten per cent

of American businesses, the industries in which black ownership is concentrated, like services or social assistance, are the most severely affected
by the lockdown. These combined effects mean that black populations
will take much longer to recover from the debilitating effects of Covid-19
and the ensuing economic crisis than their white counterparts.

From a social reproduction perspective, then, it is not the pre-existing medical conditions of the individual, but rather decades of
socio-economic marginalisation that cause elevated Covid-19 vulnerability. The historical exclusion of African Americans from high income
brackets amounts to a clear social-reproductive disadvantage, visible in
everything from general health and life-expectancy to living standards.
A social reproduction approach to Covid-19 links the vulnerability of
African Americans to the combined histories of health and inequality.
In this view, living lives locked out of labour markets creates disproportionate vulnerability to chronic illness, which in turn facilitates more
severe forms of Covid-19. Bearing in mind that race and class-specific
deprivations are passed down through the generations, the low socioeconomic status of African Americans represents a health risk so stark as
to constitute a clear biopolitical disadvantage. In this sense, it is not just,
as Stuart Hall claimed, that 'race is the modality in which class is lived'
(1978:394). Rather, we should say with Ruth Wilson Gilmore that race is
what determines 'vulnerability to premature death' (2002:261).

As the production of endemic racial disadvantage met with the
explosion of the Coronavirus, this vulnerability was only augmented.
However, when on 25 May 2020, an unarmed black man was suffocated
by a white police officer in Minneapolis, events took an unexpected
turn. Following the murder of George Floyd, protests erupted across the
country, not only demanding justice for the murder victim, but making
the explicit link between Coronavirus vulnerability and racialised police
violence.

Beginning locally the day after the assassination, the protests soon
spread to over 2000 American cities. Thousands of people marched in
solidarity, occupied squares and voiced their dissent. In some cities,
demonstrators burned cars, looted shops and removed or defaced statues
of Confederate leaders. Marshalling a predictably militarised response
to the civil unrest, the Trump administration deployed over 62,000
National Guard troops to support local police (Kim, 2020: para. 5) and
arrested at least 14,000 people for skirmishes with law enforcement
(Pham, 2020: para. 1). By 3 June, over 200 cities had imposed curfews

to delegitimise night-time demonstrations (Warren and Hadden, 2020: para. 1). However, the activists proved remarkably resilient to the state's containment measures. Recent polls estimate that as of 3 July, the George Floyd killing brought between 15 and 26 million people into the streets, making this the largest mass protest in US history (Buchanan, Bui & Patel, 2020: para. 1).

Beyond their scale, what is remarkable about the uprisings is that protesters consistently connected police brutality to Coronavirus vulnerability, as part of the same systemic exposure to premature death that characterises everyday life for black Americans. As Baltimore activist Rajikh Hayes told a *New York Times* reporter, 'It's really a simple question: Am I going to let a disease kill me or am I going to let the system – the police [. . .] And if something is going to take me out when I don't have a job, which one do I prefer' (cited in Gay Stolberg, 2020: para. 4).

Indeed, comparing the figures on black mortality from Covid-19 and from police violence, the overlap between the two is uncanny. Black Americans constitute 13 per cent of the US population, yet they make up 24 per cent of Coronavirus deaths (Gramlich and Funk, 2020: para. 2) and 26 per cent of the victims of police killings (Clegg, 2016:335). On average, white Americans are two times less likely to die from Coronavirus (Hlavinka, 2020: para. 2) and 2.5 times less likely to be shot by police (Clegg, 2016:335). Ultimately, these figures elide the difference between unforeseen disaster and endemic social crisis. What remains are the vulnerability factors that are imprinted onto populations and that accompany individual and collective lifetimes from the cradle to the (often untimely) grave.

The George Floyd protests derived much of their force by drawing attention to the identity of disaster and crisis – or of Coronavirus vulnerability and exposure to police violence. This generalised vulnerability should not be read merely as a consequence of direct racism in the medical sector or in law enforcement (though this surely adds to the problem). Instead, it bespeaks the social-reproductive disadvantage of black populations in the USA. Diminished capacities for social reproduction are the outcome of a decades-long process of economic marginalisation that has excluded black Americans from the mechanisms of intergenerational wealth transmission that many white families benefitted from in the post-war era. The George Floyd demonstrations expressed this. Rather than merely campaigning for police reform, they were the first protests to call out and oppose the sum total of accumulated social vulnerability: to illness, to poverty, to crime and to the police.

Considering the relationship between disaster and revolt from 2012 to 2020, the recent wave of uprisings is the mirror image of the protests that opened the decade. While the disastrous event of Superstorm Sandy transformed the political demands of Occupy into self-organised disaster relief – of the kind so easily co-opted by the state – the killing of George Floyd fused a series of scattered mutual aid initiatives into a coherent movement, plunging the state into crisis. In the aftermath of Superstorm Sandy, the prefigurative potential of community-led social reproduction remained symbolic, in its failure to challenge state power. With Coronavirus, on the other hand, we experience the limits of the current configuration of social reproduction – shared as it is between the state, the market and civil-society. While in 2012, the false universality of disaster pacified political protest, now, the combined and uneven effects of natural and man-made disaster reveal the urgency of political change, for which the struggle continues.

Notes

1. The number of victims of Hurricane Katrina is a contested issue. This is mostly due to the large number of agencies from the Federal Emergency Management Agency to the National Oceanic and Atmospheric Administration and the Department of Health in Louisiana that compiled their own data in the aftermath of the disaster. Although 1,836 is an often-cited number of overall deaths from the hurricane, none of the above agencies has actually endorsed it. For a statistical overview, see (Plyer, 2016).

2. When speaking of civil society in the following, I use the term in its Marxist sense to designate the aggregate social sphere that stands opposed to the state. In the disaster context, this includes NGOs, faith-based and political organisations, as well as formal and informal community organisations. For an overview of Marx's opposition between the state and civil society, see (Draper, 1977; Draper, 1986).

3. For Marx, it is with the spread of capitalist agriculture in the nineteenth century that the disruption of humanity's social metabolism with nature first becomes apparent. At the time, Europe and North America experienced a profound agricultural crisis, caused by persistent over-farming, leading to a drop in soil quality, due to the depletion of the soil-nutrient cycle. For Marx, the crisis in agriculture becomes a case in point for capitalism's inability to maintain the resources that it uses. While the crisis of fertility could be overcome with the invention of chemical fertiliser, this has only further exacerbated the metabolic rift by drastically increasing toxic waste in the soil. One capitalist disaster thus begets another. For an overview of Marx's metabolic rift, see (Foster, 1999).

4. This circumstantial critique has today become common currency even with the global business elite. Electric car manufacturers, such as Tesla have built their entire business model around the notion of the green economy and even oil companies like Royal Dutch Shell pledge to reduce the carbon footprint of their energy products. These practices have increasingly come under critical scrutiny under the heading of 'greenwashing'. For a critical overview, see (Greer and Bruno, 1997).

5. When speaking of community in the following, I use the term in its widest acceptation to designate an informal body of groups and individuals. Located below civil society, community members are often informal and un-organised. However, community activities also form the building blocks of civil society initiatives if they pass into the public sphere, thereby receiving political recognition.

6. From 1803 to 1950, the federal government provided relief in over 100 disaster situations, gradually becoming the primary actor to administer aid

during emergencies. See Chapter 2 on federalising disaster aid in (Farber and Chen, 2006:24–53).

7. The neologism stagflation refers to the 1970s recession, which saw the simultaneous presence of both stagnation, or low economic growth and inflation, i.e. rising prices, an anomaly in the economic landscape. The coupling of low growth, resulting in high unemployment and rising prices led to a drastic crisis in the ability of people to reproduce their lives and livelihoods.

8. Austerity emerged in the United Kingdom during WWII to justify the rationing of food following a wartime logic of necessity. As such, it was laden with the moral injunction that patriotic citizens should accept the state's rationing for the benefit of the greater good and the nation. For a history of austerity internationally and in the US, see (Blyth, 2013).

9. In political economics, the commons denotes a resource, owned and managed not by the market or the state, but by a self-organised, politically autonomous unit. Harking back to medieval England's use of so-called common land, the term is today used in a wide sense, encompassing claims to the free use of urban space, as well as digital infrastructures and natural resources. Key to the commons is the idea of liberating resources of their exchange value, promoted by private ownership and to return them to the common use of the community. For an overview, see (Linnebaugh, 2008; Federici, 2018).

10. In his article, 'War against the Center,' Peter Galison argues that it was the vulnerability of centralised structures to bombing that caused the American suburban sprawl, as well as the planned distribution of vital infrastructures across the country and even underground. See (Galison, 2001:7–33).

11. The anthropologists Gregory Bateson and Margaret Mead contrasted Wiener's first order cybernetics with their own new brand of second-order cybernetics. Modelling itself on biology and living organisms, rather than on machines and on physics. This new cybernetics elaborated sophisticated accounts of decentralised, open systems, in which the system's observer always directly affects the system itself. For an account of the transition to second order cybernetics, see (Von Foerster, 2003). Despite its self-description as emancipatory and anti-hierarchical, recent research has demonstrated how political control persists and even flourishes after decentralisation. See (Galloway, 2004; Lazzarato, 2014).

12. Chris Russill and Chad Lavin have explored how the tipping point metaphor was used during Hurricane Katrina to separate a pre-disaster ordinary from the alleged onset of social disintegration. See (Russill and Lavin, 2011:3–31). I have discussed the tipping point concept further in relation to outbreak and contagion narratives in disasters. See (Illner and Holm, 2015:51–64).

13. This is the title of a 2014 monograph by the disaster scholar, Kathleen Tierney (Tierney, 2014). While Tierney was strongly advocating resilience in this book, she has had a recent, if somewhat perplexing change of heart. In a 2015 article, she offers a critique of the concept. See (Tierney, 2015:1327–42).

14. Among Marxist feminists, another key critique of WfH targeted the group's claim that domestic labour was directly productive of value. In the 1970s, social reproduction feminism was split between the WfH camp, that drew on Italian autonomous Marxism to frame housework as capitalistically value-producing, and their critics who, based on a reading of Marx's *Capital*, conceptualised domestic labour as unproductive of value. Stemming from their diverging analysis, the two schools of thought developed radically different political strategies. While the Autonomist school emphasised the need to withdraw from capitalist social relations in order to develop revolutionary commons, in which people would reproduce their lives non-capitalistically, their critics, whom Susan Ferguson calls the 'Marxian School' called on social movements to struggle against capitalism from within. For an incisive review of the so-called domestic labour debate, see (Ferguson, 2020:120–39).

15. In another important contribution to social reproduction feminism, Lise Vogel displaced housework from the centre of the debate, arguing instead for a structural relation between productive and unproductive labour, in which value-producing labour always relied on non-capitalist externalities to function. See (Vogel, 2013).

16. While the distinction between public sphere and private sphere can be narrated in different ways, many scholars have traced its origin to legal and political transformations in the sixteenth and seventeenth centuries. With the rise of the nation-state, and conceptions of national sovereignty, there arose a necessity to think of the state as the guarantor of a particularly public realm. See (Horwitz, 1982:1423–8). Following Gonzales and Neton, I argue for an understanding of the public as a mechanism by which the state formally recognises social activity, thereby bestowing value onto it. For Gonzales and Neton, echoing Marx 'the public is an abstration from society in the form of the state. This sphere of the political and the juridical is the real abstraction of Right separated from the actual divisions and differences constituting civil society' (2014:159). The public is thus an idealised sphere, in which private individuals encounter each other as equal citizens, 'even though in "real life" (the private sphere of civil society), they are anything but' (ibid.). Applied to our context of social reproduction, we can say that by recognising the DMM and the waged IMM spheres as formally performing reproductive labour, the state elevates these reproductive activities into the public realm, thereby pushing the unwaged IMM or abject spheres of community-led social reproduction into the private realm.

17. Tracy Revels outlines how the extensive federal investment into Key West in particular and Florida tourism in general made Florida the first US state to exit the Great Depression. See (Revels, 2011:130–31).

18. This dual role of providing a public service, while advancing economic interests is the crux of state-led social reproduction. The potential reconcilability between capital and labour interests was the mantra of Keynesianism and of many Western states after WWII, investing heavily into state-led public services. However, even before the advent of neoliberalism, which steered

state intervention into increasingly market-mediated waters, American infrastructural development is proof of the overbearing weight of capital concerns in state-led social reproduction projects in the entire twentieth century.

19. Early Florida tourism took place within a context of rampant racism in which blacks were not allowed to enter white leisure facilities even if they could afford them. The 1920s thus saw the development of a separate African American tourist industry, particularly at American Beach, north of Jacksonville.

20. In the context of California, Mike Davis has outlined how after the federalisation of disaster aid, poor taxpayers in the Midwest were made to pay for the reconstruction of holiday homes in Malibu. In line with Ted Steinberg's critique of the way in which federal funds were used to subsidise real estate development in highly disaster-prone regions, Davis explains how 'by declaring Malibu a federal disaster area and offering blaze victims tax relief as well as preferential low-interest loans, the Eisenhower administration established the precedent for the public subsidisation of firebelt suburbs' (Davis, 1995:1–36, here p. 8).

21. In his book *The Global Slump*, David McNally contradicts Robert Brenner's argument of an uninterrupted economic downturn since the 1970s, arguing that neoliberal reform ushered in a period of capitalist expansion in the 1980s that only came to an end with the 2008 collapse. Leaving disagreements on crisis dynamics by the wayside, my central claim that the economic restructuring of the 1980s was achieved on the back of workers' living standards is shared by both authors. Whether these reforms increased or reduced profit margins, they certainly severely contracted social reproduction. To review this debate, see (McNally 2011:25–60).

22. As political theorist Kevin Doogan has suggested, deindustrialisation itself did not automatically bring about social immiseration. Rather, insecurities in living standards were created by changes in labour dynamics, coupled with neoliberal policies that exposed the welfare of people increasingly to market forces. I address the neoliberal policy shifts regarding social reproduction during disasters at length in Chapters 6, 8 and 9. For this analysis, see (Doogan, 2009).

23. While the decline in manufacturing and the concomitant rise of the service sector in the 1980s is relatively uncontested, the historian Kim Moody has argued against the assumption that deindustrialisation automatically led to a weakening of working-class power. For Kim Moody, rather than decomposition, the neoliberal turn of the 1980s ushered in a period of working class recomposition, in which the logistics revolution, the turn towards lean production and the shifting of capitalism's geographical centre opened up new terrains of class struggle. While I have doubts regarding the potentials of capitalism's latest consolidation for militant labour organising, Moody agrees with me that the immediate effect of neoliberal economic restructuring is an 'increasing decline in living standards as real incomes shrink,

the social wage fades and political attacks on workers and unions increase' (2017:75).

24. The political philosopher George Caffentzis has elaborated on the idea of 'self-reproducing automata', as fulfilling capital's dream of a frictionless, self-reproducing labour force. See (Caffentzis, 1990:35–41).

25. In her book *Scenes of Subjection*, Saidiya Hartman reconstructs the transitionary period between black slavery and freedom and argues that the legal ascription of subjecthood to blacks served to make African Americans legally accountable for crimes. Against liberal equations of subjecthood and freedom, Hartman argues that full subjectivity only further constrained blacks and controversially calls into question the presumed discontinuity between freedom and slavery. See (Hartman, 1997:115–25).

26. Brady Thomas Heiner claims that Foucault's preoccupation with war in his lecture series 'Society Must Be Defended' originated in an exploration of the racial politics of the US and especially his knowledge of the Black Panther Party that he gained through Jean Genet. See (Heiner, 2007:322).

27. A worker's inquiry is an investigation of a workplace from the worker's point of view. From Marx over Trotsky to Italian operaismo, different research methodologies have been proposed to generate bottom-up knowledge of a production process, in order to adapt political strategies and tactics accordingly. The old worker's tactic of sabotage would be unthinkable without prior investigation into the production process by workers. For an overview, see (Woodcock, 2014).

28. The irreconcilability of revolution and reform has a long history in socialist thought. It was perhaps most poignantly formulated by Rosa Luxemburg in her critique of the German Social Democratic Party's Erfurt Programme from 1891. While setting out the revolutionary overthrow of capitalism as its official goal, the party simultaneously campaigned for a series of welfare reforms to ease the hardship of the working class. Critical of this dual strategy, Luxemburg opposed the Erfurt Programme by vehemently pitting revolution against reform: 'That is why people who pronounce themselves in favour of the method of legislative reform in place and in contradistinction to the conquest of political power and social revolution, do not really choose a more tranquil, calmer and slower road to the same goal, but a different goal. Our program becomes not the realization of socialism, but the reform of capitalism; not the suppression of the wage labor system but the diminution of exploitation, that is, the suppression of the abuses of capitalism instead of suppression of capitalism itself' (2008:90).

29. This episode was reported in the *Chicago Tribune*, 17 July 1995, p. (2)5.

30. I have elsewhere contextualised the effects of these demographic trends on labour markets, immigration and reproductive medicine. See (Illner, 2017:42–9).

31. Stuart Hall has masterfully shown how the cultural over-sensitisation to crime creates moral panics out of all proportion to actually existing social threats. See (Hall, Critcher, Jefferson et al., 1978:3–28).

32. In July 2014, African American Eric Garner would be arrested and strangled to death by NYPD officers because of being suspected of selling 'loosies', single cigarettes from illegally imported cartons. For Joshua Clover, this petty crime, although never officially confirmed in the case of Garner, is indicative of the informal labour adopted by disenfranchised African Americans for lack of waged work. See (Clover, 2016a).

33. In the 1980s, steel works closed *en masse* across the nation, leading to a 'steel crisis'. The largest steel manufacturer, U.S. Steel increasingly 'diversified out' of steel and began trading in chemicals, oil, gas and real estate. Today, only one third of its sales are in steel alone. For an account of American steel works closures as exemplary of deindustrialisation, see (Schulman, 1982:33–5).

34. This in itself is surprising since the city's exposure to hurricanes has drastically increased over the years. For an informed ecological history of New York City, see (Steinberg, 2014).

35. In addition, the anthropologists Stan and Paul Cox describe how during Hurricane Sandy, the official and intricate contingency plans by New York's Emergency Management were ignored and the decisive authority relegated directly to the mayor. For the authors, this episode is representative of a larger trend in emergency management that regards official disaster plans as too complex to be followed, preferring to delegate responsibility to non-specialists such as politicians and volunteers. See (Cox and Cox, 2016:73).

36. The very first study to comment on the pro-social behaviour emerging after a disaster is Samuel Henry Prince's account of the explosion in Halifax Harbour in Nova Scotia, Canada. See (Prince, 1920).

37. In this collection, the essay *From the Native's Point of View* in particular, outlines Geertz' methodology for understanding the particular knowledge of a subaltern group. See (Geertz, 1983:55–73).

38. The comparison with Marxism is incisive here. While in Marx, the proletariat is similarly radically partial in its social positioning, its epistemic privilege stems from being at the same time the only 'universal class'. Rather than from simply being embodied as partial, the proletariat ascends to knowledge through what Alberto Toscano calls its partisanship, i.e. by dynamically negating capitalist relations. For a fine account of this alternative Marxist version of partiality, see (Toscano, 2009:175–91).

39. The Homeland Security Act of 2002, passed in the direct aftermath of 9/11, united a panoply of new and old agencies in one organisation. It constituted the largest governmental reorganisation since the founding of the Department of Defense in 1947. For a view of Homeland Security and its involvement in Hurricane Sandy, see (Hintze, 2014: para. 1).

40. Indeed, Occupy's collaboration with governmental bodies such as the NYPD, as well as corporations like Home Depot, was contentiously discussed among participants of the social movement and by no means an uncontroversial issue. However, it was ruled that by collaborating with antagonistic institutions the movement would be able to extend its control and influence into areas that would have otherwise remained inaccessible.

41. This extreme reduction was only topped by the budget proposal of the Republican Party under Mitt Romney that suggested a 40% cut to the FEMA budget. See (Khimm, 2012: para. 8).

42. In 1971, President Richard Nixon uncoupled the dollar from the gold standard, making the future of the world economy dependent on the future-oriented fluctuations of the stock market. In this context, the political economist David McNally has differentiated between value and capital, arguing that Nixon's decoupling proclaimed the end of value and hailed the beginning of 'fictitious capital'. See (McNally, 2009:35–83).

43. The 'labour metaphysic' is C. Wright Mills' term from his 1960 'Letter to the New Left'. See (Wright Mills, 1960).

44. This non-commercial sphere can comprise both waged and unwaged forms of labour. Thus, a civil servant, active in state-led social reproduction will earn a salary for their labour, while an unwaged actor from civil society will not.

45. The extent of this provision varies strongly from country to country, but one finds a variaiton of state-funded IMM activities in almost all modern states.

46. This situation has given rise to a rich academic and activist debate on the possibility of organising 'the commons', spaces for the collective sharing of resources and the self-organisation of collective social reproduction. While many Marxist feminists have actively tried to self-organise social reproduction, the notion of the commons as autonomously emancipatory has been recently heavily critiqued. For a pro-commons perspective, see (Federici, 2012:138–49). For a critique of the commons discourse, see (Williams, 2011:175–95).

47. Indeed, David Cameron's idea of the Big Society, still one of the hallmarks of the Conservative government in the UK, shares a lot with the politics of self-help endorsed by the Department for Homeland Security. Cameron advocated the organisation of social services 'on a voluntary basis'. The Big Society is a political culture 'where people, in their everyday lives, in their homes, in their neighbourhoods, in their workplace [. . .] feel both free and powerful enough to help themselves and their own communities.' See (Cameron, 2010: para. 2).

48. Fassin's account of the emergence of humanitarianism as a resolutely anti-state position is complemented by Michael Behrent's brilliant study of the French Second Left. In the 1980s, the Second Left was an important side current in the French political landscape that alongside the emerging neo-liberal policymakers, critiqued the established Left's fixation on the state. Against the state's policy of dirigisme or intervention, the Second Left promoted *autogestion* or self-management to 'decompose and redistribute the functions of the capitalist state, transforming its shackles into a voluntary institution.' See Behrent, p. 96 (2015:69–155).

49. It is debatable to what extent Adams' framing of the federal government's austerity measures as a 'failure' is adequate to the situation. My case studies have demonstrated that rather than a failure, the federal withdrawal from

reproductive activities constitutes a structural tendency, rather than a failed attempt.

50. It is impossible to know the exact number of coronavirus fatalities. This is because different national health systems capture their data differently. Furthermore, many health systems experienced an acute shortage of testing capacities, making it impossible to accurately determine Covid-19 deaths. Because of these shortcomings, some public health experts have taken overall mortality rates since the outbreak of the coronavirus as more meaningful figures to determine Covid-19-related excess mortality. The following estimates are taken from the online dashboard of the Johns Hopkins University Coronavirus Research Center. Since numbers still continue to rise every day, they will fast be outdated. For up-to-date figures, see https://coronavirus.jhu.edu/map.html. For overall mortality rates statistics, see (Wu, McCann, Katz et al., 2020: fig. 1).

51. The concept of mutual aid was popularised at the turn of the century by the Russian anarchist Peter Kropotkin, who theorised cooperation and solidarity between community members as an anthropological constant that helped the human species evolve. According to Kropotkin, mutual aid was evolutionarily superior to private property, and humankind was drastically falling behind its evolutionary potential with the spread of capitalism. See (Kropotkin, 2009). While today, few would hold on to an anthropological explanation of mutual aid, the practice has remained at the forefront of radical politics throughout the twentieth century and has gained in importance with the downturn in electoral politics since the turn of the century.

52. According to official statistics, '75 percent of all frontline workers are people of color, including 82 percent of cleaning services employees. More than 40 percent of transit employees are black while over 60 percent of cleaning workers are Hispanic.' See https://comptroller.nyc.gov/reports/new-york-citys-frontline-workers.

Bibliography

Adams, V. (2012). 'The Other Road to Serfdom: Recovery by the Market and the Affect Economy in New Orleans.' *Public Culture* 24(1): 185–216.

Adams, V. (2013). *Markets of Sorrow, Labors of Faith: New Orleans in the Wake of Katrina*. London; Durham, Duke University Press.

Ambinder, E., D. M. Jennings, I. Blachman-Biatch, K. Edgemon, P. Hull and A. Taylor. (2013). 'The Resilient Social Network.' *Homeland Security*. http:// homelandsecurity.org/docs/the resilient social network.pdf. (last accessed December 2019).

Aradau, C. and R. v. Munster. (2011). *Politics of Catastrophe: Genealogies of the Unknown*. London; New York, Routledge.

Arena, J. (2012). *Driven from New Orleans: How Nonprofits Betray Public Housing and Promote Privatization*. Minneapolis, University of Minnesota Press.

Arrighi, G. (1994). *The Long Twentieth Century: Money, Power, and the Origins of Our Times*. London; New York, Verso.

Bankoff, G. (2004). 'The Historical Geography of Disaster: "Vulnerability" and "Local Knowledge" in Western Discourse.' in *Mapping Vulnerability: Disasters, Development, and People*. Bankoff, G., G. Frerks and D. Hilhorst. London; Sterling, VA, Earthscan Publications: 25–36.

Bankoff, G. and D. Hilhorst. (2004). 'Introduction: Mapping Vulnerability.' in *Mapping Vulnerability: Disasters, Development, and People*. G. Bankoff, G. Frerks and D. Hilhorst. London; Sterling, VA, Earthscan Publications: 1–10.

Bankoff, G., G. Frerks and D. Hilhorst. (2004). *Mapping Vulnerability: Disasters, Development, and People*. London; Sterling, VA, Earthscan Publications.

Barr, M. (2012). 'Occupy Wall Street morphs into Occupy Sandy, Offering Relief.' The Denver Post. www.denverpost.com/ci_21973563/occupy-wall-street-morphs-into-occupy-sandy-offering. (last accessed March 2016).

Barusch, A. S. (2011). 'Disaster, Vulnerability, and Older Adults: Toward a Social Work Response.' *Journal of Gerontological Social Work*, 54(4):347–50.

Behrent, M. C. (2015). 'Liberalism without Humanism: Michel Foucault and the Free Market Creed, 1976–1979.' in *Foucault and neoliberalism*. D. Zamora and M. C. Behrent. Malden, Mass., Polity Press: 69–155.

Bhattacharya, T. (2017). 'Introduction. Mapping Social Reproduction Theory.' in *Social Reproduction Theory. Remapping Class, Recentering Oppression*. T. Bhattacharya. London, Pluto Press: 1–20.

Black Panther Party (2007) [1972], 'The Black Panther Party Program March 29, 1972 Platform.' *The Black Panther*. D. Hilliard. New York, Atria Books.

Blaikie, P. M., T. Cannon, I. Davis and B. Wisner (1994). *At Risk: Natural Hazards, People's Vulnerability, and Disasters*. London; New York, Routledge.

Blaikie, P. M., T. Cannon, I. Davis and B. Wisner (2004). *At Risk: Natural Hazards, People's Vulnerability, and Disasters*. second edition. London; New York, Routledge.

Bloom, J. and W. E. Martin (2013). *Black Against Empire: The History and Politics of the Black Panther Party*. Berkeley, University of California Press.

Blyth, M. (2013). *Austerity: the History of a Dangerous Idea*. Oxford; New York, Oxford University Press.

Bonanno, G. A., S. Galea, A. Bucciarelli and D. Vlahov (2006). 'Psychological Resilience after Disaster: New York City in the Aftermath of the September 11th Terrorist Attack.' *Psychological Science* 17(3): 181–86.

Brenner, R. (2006). *The Economics of Global Turbulence: The Advanced Capitalist Economies from Long Boom to Long Downturn, 1945–2005*. London; New York, Verso.

Brockwell, S., F. Kilminster and A. Starr-Bochiccio. (2009). 'A Red Hook Community Health Assessment.' *Red Hook Community Health Needs and Assets Assessment*. www.brooklyncb6.org/_attachments/2009-05-22%20RHI%20Red%20Hook%20Houses%20Health%20Assessment.pdf. (last accessed December 2019).

Brunkard, J., G. Namulanda and R. Ratard (2008). 'Hurricane Katrina Deaths, Louisiana, 2005.' *Disaster Medicine and Public Health Preparedness* 2(4): 215–23.

Brunsma, D. L. (2010). *The Sociology of Katrina, Perspectives on a Modern Catastrophe*. Lanham, Rowman & Littlefield.

Buchanan, L., Q. Bui and J.K. Patel (2020). 'Black Lives Matter May Be the Largest Movement in U.S. History.' *New York Times*. www.nytimes.com/interactive/2020/07/03/us/george-floyd-protests-crowd-size.html (last accessed July 2020).

Burnett, G. M. (1986). *Florida's Past: People and Events that Shaped the State*. Englewood, Fla., Pineapple Press.

Burton, I. and R. W. Kates (1964). 'The Perception of Natural Hazards in Resource Management.' *Natural Resources Journal* 3(3): 412–41.

Burton, I., R. W. Kates and G. F. White (1993). *The Environment as Hazard*. New York, Guilford Press.

Caffentzis, G. (1990). 'On Africa and Self-Reproducing Automata.' *Midnight Notes* 10: 35–41.

Cameron, D. (2010). Speech 'The Big Society', Liverpool, 19 July 2010. The UK Government. www.gov.uk/government/speeches/big-society-speech (last accessed December 2019).

Carlin, M. and S. Federici. (2014). 'The Exploitation of Women, Social Reproduction, and the Struggle against Global Capital.' *Theory & Event*. https://muse.jhu.edu/journals/theory_and_event/v017/17.3.carlin.html. (last accessed June 2017).

Caygill, H. (2013). 'Philosophy and the Black Panthers.' *Radical Philosophy* 179: 7–14.

Center for Disease Control and Prevention (2020). 'People of Any Age with Underlying Medical Conditions.' CDC. www.cdc.gov/coronavirus/2019-ncov/

need-extra-precautions/people-with-medical-conditions.html (last accessed July 2020).

Chandler, A. D. (1977). *The Visible Hand.* Cambridge, MA, Harvard University Press.

Charles, K. K.; E. Hurst and M. Schwartz (2018) 'The Transformation of Manufacture and the Decline in U.S. Employment.' *NBER Working Paper Series.* Working Paper 24468: 1–69.

Cisneros, H. and L. Engdahl (2009). *From Despair to Hope, HOPE VI and the New Promise of Public Housing in America's Cities.* Washington, D.C, Brookings Institution Press.

Cleeland, N. (2020). 'Hospitals Face Staffing Shortages, Reduced Budgets in Coronavirus Pandemic.' SHRM. www.shrm.org/resourcesandtools/hr-topics/employee-relations/pages/hospitals-face-staffing-shortages-reduced-budgets-in-coronavirus-pandemic.aspx (last accessed July 2020).

Clegg, J. (2016). 'A Class Blind Spot? Anti-racism in the United States.' *Global Labour Journal* 7(3): 334–43.

Clover, J. (2016a). 'Riot Strike Riot Book Launch.' *Vancouver, SFU's Vancity Office for Community Engagement.* www.sfu.ca/video-library/video/1624/view.html (last accessed January 2020).

Clover, J. (2016b). *Riot. Strike. Riot.: The New Era of Uprisings.* London; New York, Verso.

Coats, D. R. (2019). 'Worldwide Threat Assessment of the U.S. Intelligence Community.' Office of the Director of National Intelligence. www.dni.gov/files/ODNI/documents/2019-ATA-SFR---SSCI.pdf (last accessed July 2020).

Comfort, L. K., A. Boin and C. C. Demchak (2010). *Designing Resilience: Preparing for Extreme Events.* Pittsburgh, Pa., University of Pittsburgh Press.

Cooper, A. and E. Smith. (2011). 'Homicide Trends in the United States, 1980–2008.' *Bureau of Justice Statistics.* https://web.archive.org/web/20180330165915/https://www.bjs.gov/index.cfm?ty=pbdetail&iid=2221 (last accessed December 2016).

Cox, S. and P. Cox (2016). *How the World Breaks: Life in Catastrophe's Path from the Carribean to Siberia.* New York, The New Press.

Cutter, S., J. A. Ahern, B. Amadei et al. (2013). 'Disaster Resilience: A National Imperative.' *Environment: Science and Policy for Sustainable Development* 55(2): 25–9.

Dalla Costa, M. and S. James (1975). *The Power of Women and the Subversion of the Community.* Bristol, Falling Wall Press Ltd.

Dauber, M. L. (2013). *The Sympathetic State: Disaster Relief and the Origins of the American Welfare State.* Chicago, University of Chicago Press.

Davis, M. (1995). 'The Case for Letting Malibu Burn.' *Environmental History Review* 19(2): 1–36.

Davis, M. (1998). *Ecology of Fear: Los Angeles and the Imagination of Disaster.* New York, Metropolitan Books.

Davis, M. (2002). *Dead Cities, and Other Tales.* New York, The New Press.

Denning, M. (2004). *Culture in the Age of Three Worlds.* London; New York, Verso.

Diavolo, L. (2020). 'People Are Fighting the Coronavirus With Mutual Aid Efforts to Help Each Other. *Teen Vogue*. www.teenvogue.com/story/people-fighting-coronavirus-mutual-aid-efforts-help-each-other (last accessed July 2020).

Doogan, K. (2009). *New Capitalism? The Transformation of Work*. Cambridge, Polity.

Draper, H. (1977). *Karl Marx's Theory of Revolution Vol. 1: State and Bureaucracy*. New York, Monthly Review Press.

Draper, H. (1986). *Karl Marx's Theory of Revolution Vol. 2: The Politics of Social Classes*. New York, Monthly Review Press.

Duneier, M. (2004). 'Scrutinizing the Heat: On Ethnic Myths and the Importance of Shoe Leather.' *Contemporary Sociology* 33(2): 139–50.

Dynes, R. R. (1994). 'Community Emergency Planning: False Assumptions and Inappropriate Analogies.' *International Journal of Mass Emergencies and Disasters* 12(2): 141–58.

Easterling, K. (2014). *Extrastatecraft: the Power of Infrastructure Space*. London; New York, Verso.

Economist Briefing. 'Falling Short. The Trouble with Pensions.' *Economist* (12 June 2008). www.economist.com/briefing/2008/06/12/falling-short. (last accessed December 2019).

Economist editorial. 'Black Lives Live Longer.' *Economist* (15 June 2019). www.economist.com/united-states/2019/06/15/black-men-in-america-are-living-almost-as-long-as-white-men (last accessed December 2019).

Edelman, S. (2020). 'Two pols urge de Blasio to oust Health Commissioner Barbot over coronavirus response.' *New York Post*. https://nypost.com/2020/04/04/nyc-pols-urge-de-blasio-to-oust-health-commissioner-over-coronavirus-response/ (last accessed July 2020).

Eisen L-B and O. Roeder. (2015). 'America's Faulty Perception of Crime Rates.' *The Brennan Center*. www.brennancenter.org/our-work/analysis-opinion/americas-faulty-perception-crime-rates. (last accessed December 2019).

Enarson, E. P. (2012). *Women Confronting Natural Disaster: From Vulnerability to Resilience*, Boulder, CO., Lynne Rienner Publishers.

Endnotes editorial. (2015). 'Brown v. Ferguson.' *Endnotes* 4: 10–70 (October 2015).

Endnotes editorial. (2015b). 'A History of Separation.' *Endnotes* 4: 70–194 (October 2015).

Farber, D. A. and J. Chen (2006). *Disasters and the Law: Katrina and Beyond*. New York, Aspen Publishers.

Fassin, D. (2010). 'Heart of Humaneness: The Moral Economy of Humanitarian Intervention.' in *Contemporary states of emergency: the politics of military and humanitarian interventions*. D. Fassin and M. Pandolfi. New York; Cambridge, Mass., Zone Books; Distributed by the MIT Press: 269–93.

Fassin, D. (2012). *Humanitarian Reason: A Moral History of the Present Times*. Berkeley, University of California Press.

Federici, S. (2012). *Revolution at Point Zero: Housework, Reproduction, and Feminist Struggle*. Oakland, CA; Brooklyn, NY; London, PM Press; Autonomedia.

Federici, S. (2018). *Re-enchanting the World: Feminism and the Politics of the Commons*. Oakland, CA., PM Press.

Feeney, S. A. (2012). 'Disabled People especially vulnerable in calamities such as Sandy.' *AM New York*. www.amny.com/urbanite-1.812039/disabled-people-especially-vulnerable-in-calamities-such-as-sandy (last accessed December 2019).

Ferguson, S. (2020). *Women and Work*. London, Pluto Press.

Ferguson, S. and D. McNally (2013). 'Capital, Labour-Power, and Gender-Relations: Introduction to the Historical Materialism Edition of Marxism and the Oppression of Women.' in *Marxism and the Oppression of Women: Toward a Unitary Theory*. L. Vogel. Leiden, Brill: xvii–xl.

Flamm, M. W. (2017). *In the Heat of the Summer: The New York Riots of 1964 and the War on Crime*. Philadelphia, PA., University of Pennsylvania Press.

Foster, J. B. (1999). 'Marx's Theory of Metabolic Rift: Classical Foundations for Environmental Sociology.' *American Journal of Sociology* 105(2): 366–405.

Fraser, N. (2017). 'Crisis of Care? On the Social-Reproductive Contradictions of Contemporary Capitalism.' in *Social Reproduction Theory. Remapping Class, Recentering Oppression*. T. Bhattacharya. London, Pluto Press: 21–36.

Fritz, C. E. (1996). 'Disasters and Mental Health: Therapeutic Principles Drawn From Disaster Studies.' *Historical And Comparative Disaster Series*. http://udspace.udel.edu/bitstream/handle/19716/1325/HC 10.pdf?sequenc. (last accessed March 2020).

Frontline (2005). 'A Short History of FEMA.' *Frontline*. www.pbs.org/wgbh/pages/frontline/storm/etc/femahist.html (last accessed July 2019).

Fussell, E., N. Sastry and M. VanLandingham (2010). 'Race, Socioeconomic Status, and Return Migration to New Orleans after Hurricane Katrina.' *Population and Environment* 31(1-3): 20–42.

Galison, P. (1994). 'The Ontology of the Enemy: Norbert Wiener and the Cybernetic Vision.' *Critical Inquiry* 21(1): 228–66.

Galison, P. (2001). 'War against the Center.' *Grey Room* 4: 5–33.

Galloway, A. R. (2004). *Protocol: How Control Exists after Decentralization*. Cambridge, Mass., MIT Press.

Gay Stolberg, S. (2020). 'Pandemic within a Pandemic: Coronavirus and Police Brutality Roil Black Communities.' *New York Times*. www.nytimes.com/2020/06/07/us/politics/blacks-coronavirus-police-brutality.html (last accessed July 2020).

Geertz, C. (1983). *Local Knowledge: Further Essays in Interpretive Anthropology*. New York, Basic Books.

Genet, J. and B. Bray (2003). *Prisoner of Love*. New York, New York Review Books.

Goldner, L. (2007). 'Fictitious Capital for Beginners.' *Mute Magazine* 2(6): 52–72.

Goldner, L. (2013). 'Fictitious Capital and Contracted Social Reproduction Today: China and Permanent Revolution.' *Mute Magazine*. www.metamute.

org/editorial/articles/fictitious-capital-and-contracted-social-reproduction-today-china-and-permanent-revolution (last accessed December 2019).

Gonzales, M. A. and J. Neton. (2014). 'The Logic of Gender: On the Separation of Spheres and the Process of Abjection.' in *Contemporary Marxist Theory: A Reader*. A. Pendakis, J. Diamanti, N. Brown, J. Robinson and I. Szeman. New York; London, Bloomsbury Academic: 149–74.

Goodman, A., (2015). 'If You are Poor, It's Like the Hurricane Just Happened: Malik Rahim on Katrina 10 Years After.' *Democracy Now*. www.democracy-now.org/2015/8/27/if_you_are_poor_its_like, Minute 49.02 (last accessed January 2016).

Gould, E. and V. Wilson (2020). 'Black Workers face two of the most lethal preex-isting conditions for coronavirus – racism and economic inequality.' *Economic Policy Institute*. www.epi.org/publication/black-workers-covid/ (last accessed July 2020).

Graff, A. (2020). 'Tweets show SF and NYC mayors' drastically different approaches to outbreak.' *SF Gate*. www.sfgate.com/bayarea/article/de-Blasio-London-Breed-tweets-coronavirus-March-2-15189898.php (last accessed July 2020).

Gramlich, J. and C. Funk (2020). 'Black Americans face higher COVID-19 risks, are more hesitant to trust medical scientists, get vaccinated.' *Pew Research Center*. www.pewresearch.org/fact-tank/2020/06/04/black-americans-face-higher-covid-19-risks-are-more-hesitant-to-trust-medical-scientists-get-vaccinated/ (last accessed July 2020).

Greer, J. and K. Bruno. (1997). *Greenwash. The Reality behind Corporate Environ-mentalism*. Lanham, Rowman & Littlefield.

Guha Sapir, D., P. Hoyois and R. Below. (2015). *Annual Disaster Statistical Review*, Brussels, Centre for Research on the Epidemiology of Disasters.

Habermas, J. (1989). *The Structural Transformation of the Public Sphere: An Inquiry into a Category of Bourgeois Society*. Cambridge, Mass., MIT Press.

Hall, S., C. Critcher, T. Jefferson, J. Clarke and B. Roberts (1978). *Policing the Crisis: Mugging, the State, and Law and Order*. London, Macmillan.

Haraway, D. (1988). 'Situated Knowledges: The Science Question in Feminism and the Privilege of Partial Perspective.' *Feminist Studies* 14(3): 575–99.

Haraway, D. (1991). *Simians, Cyborgs and Women. The Reinvention of Nature*. London; New York, Routledge.

Harrington, M. (1962). *The Other America; Poverty in the United States*. New York, Macmillan.

Hartman, S. V. (1997). *Scenes of Subjection: Terror, Slavery, and Self-Making in Nineteenth-Century America*. New York, Oxford University Press.

Hartmann, T. (2020). 'Privatization May Be Killing Us: Mystery of Why the Trump Administration Still Hasn't Sent Out Promised Million CV Tests, as Delay is Faciliating Transmission of the Virus by Undeteceted Carriers.' *Buzzflash*. https://buzzflash.com/articles/privatization-may-be-killing-us-mystery-of-why-the-trump-administration-still-hasnt-sent-out-promised-million-cv-tests-as-delay-is-facilitating-transmission-of-the-virus-by-undetected-carriers (last accessed July 2020).

Harvey, D. (2005). *A Brief History of Neoliberalism*. Oxford; New York, Oxford University Press.

Heiner, B. T. (2007). 'Foucault and the Black Panthers.' *City* 11(3): 313–56.

Herman, M. A. (2013). *Summer of Rage. An Oral History of the 1967 Newark and Detroit Riots*. New York, Peter Lang Publishing.

Hernandez, R. (2018). 'The Fall of Employment in the Manufacturing Sector.' *U.S Bureau of Labor Statistics*. www.bls.gov/opub/mlr/2018/beyond-bls/pdf/the-fall-of-employment-in-the-manufacturing-sector.pdf (last accessed December 2019).

Hewitt, K. (1983). *Interpretations of Calamity from the Viewpoint of Human Ecology*. Boston, Mass., Allen & Unwin.

Hewitt, K. (1997). *Regions of Risk: A Geographical Introduction to Disasters*. Harlow, Longman.

Hilhorst, D. (2004). 'Complexity and Diversity: Unlocking Social Domains of Disaster Response.' in *Mapping Vulnerability: Disasters, Development, and People*. G. Bankoff, G. Frerks and D. Hilhorst. London; Sterling, VA., Earthscan Publications: 52–67.

Hilliard, D. and Huey P. Newton Foundation. (2008). *The Black Panther Party: Service to the People Programs*. Albuquerque, NM., University of New Mexico Press.

Hinton, E. (2015). '"A War Within Our Own Boundaries." Lyndon Johnson's Great Society and the Rise of the Carceral State.' *Journal of American History* 102(1): 100–112.

Hintze, T. (2014). 'Homeland Security Study Praises Occupy Sandy, With Murky Intentions.' *Truthout*. www.truth-out.org/news/item/22837-dhs-study-praises-occupy-sandy-with-murky-intentions. (last accessed December 2019).

Hlavinka, E. (2020). 'COVID-19 Killing African Americans at Shocking Rates.' *MEDPAGE TODAY*. www.medpagetoday.com/infectiousdisease/covid19/86266 (last accessed July 2020).

Holm, I. (2012). 'The Cultural Analysis of Disaster.' in *The Cultural Life of Catastrophes and Crises*. C. Meiner and K. Veel. Berlin, de Gruyter: 15–32.

Homeland Security (2013). 'Fiscal Year 2013 Congressional Justification.' The Department of Homeland Security. www.fema.gov/pdf/about/budget/11f_fema_disaster_relief_fund_dhs_fy13_cj.pdf (last accessed December 2019).

Horwitz, M. J. (1982). 'The History of the Public/Private Distinction.' *University of Pennsylvania Law Review* 130(6): 1423–8.

Iklé, F. C. (1951). 'The Effects of War Destruction upon the Ecology of Cities.' *Social Forces* 29: 383–91.

Illner, P. (2017). 'The Ebb and Flow of Gender.' *Real Review* 4: 42–9.

Illner, P. and I. Holm (2015). 'Making Sense of Disaster.' in *Disaster Research. Multidisciplinary and International Perspectives*. R. Dahlberg, O. Rubin and M. T. Vendelø. London; New York, Routledge: 51–64.

Jacobs, A., M. Richtel and M. Baker (2020). 'At War With No Ammo: Doctors Say Shortage of Protective Gear is Dire.' *New York Times*. www.nytimes.com/2020/03/19/health/coronavirus-masks-shortage.html (last accessed July 2020).

Jaffe, S. (2012). 'Occupy and the Police needn't be enemies – as Sandy showed.' *The Guardian*. www.theguardian.com/commentisfree/2012/dec/10/occupy-police-enemies-sandy. (last accessed December 2019).

James, R. (2015). *Resilience & Melancholy: Pop Music, Feminism, Neoliberalism*. Winchester, Zero Books.

James, S. (1976). *Women, the Unions, and Work: Or, What is Not to be Done, and The Perspective of Winning*. London; Bristol, Wages for Housework Women's Centre, Falling Wall Press.

Jameson, F. and S. Žižek (2016). *An American Utopia: Dual Power and the Universal Army*. London; New York, Verso.

Joseph, M. L., R. J. Chaskin and H. S. Webber (2007). 'The Theoretical Basis for Addressing Poverty Through Mixed-Income Development.' *Urban Affairs Review* 42(3): 369–409.

Juengel, S. J. (2009). 'The early novel and catastrophe.' *Novel: A Forum on Fiction* 42(3): 443–50.

Kaplan. S. (2017). 'Violent Crime is up some, but still well off historical highs.' *The Poynter Institute*. www.politifact.com/truth-o-meter/statements/2017/dec/04/jeff-sessions/violent-crime-some-still-well-historical-highs/ (last accessed December 2019).

Keith, V. M., and D. P. Smith. (1988). 'The Current Differential in Black and White Life Expectancy.' *Demography* 25(4): 625–32.

Kelman, I., T. R. Burns and N. Machado des Johansson (2015). 'Islander innovation: A research and action agenda on local responses to global issues.' *Journal Of Marine And Island Cultures* 4(1): 34–41.

Khimm, S. (2012). 'Obama cuts FEMA funding by 3 percent. Romney-Ryan cuts it by 40 percent. Or more. Or less.' *Washington Post*. www.washington post.com/news/wonk/wp/2012/10/30/obama-cuts-fema-funding-by-3-percent-romney-ryan-cuts-it-by-40-percent-or-more-or-less/. (last accessed December 2019).

Kilkenny, A. (2013). 'Occupy Sandy: One Year Later.' *The Nation*. www.thena-tion.com/article/occupy-sandy-one-year-later/. (last accessed March 2016).

Kim, S. (2020). 'Protests Near Me – List of Cities Rioting, States Where National Guard Has Been Deployed.' *Newsweek*. www.newsweek.com/protests-near-melist-cities-rioting-states-where-national-guard-has-been-deployed-1507770 (last accessed July 2020).

Klein, N. (2007). *The Shock Doctrine: The Rise of Disaster Capitalism*. New York, Metropolitan Books/Henry Holt.

Klinenberg, E. (1999). 'Denaturalizing Disaster: A Social Autopsy of the 1995 Chicago Heat Wave.' *Theory and Society* 28(2): 239–95.

Klinenberg, E. (2002). *Heat Wave: A Social Autopsy of Disaster in Chicago*. Chicago, IL., University of Chicago Press.

Knight, S. (2014). 'Occupy Sandy and the Future of Socialism.' *Truthout*. www.truth-out.org/opinion/item/22880-occupy-sandy-and-the-future-of-socialism. (last accesed March 2016).

Kropotkin, P. (2009) [1904]. *Mutual Aid, A Factor of Evolution*. New York, Cosimo Classics.

Laska, S. and B. H. Morrow (2006). 'Social vulnerabilities and Hurricane Katrina: An Unnatural Disaster in New Orleans.' *Marine Technology Society Journal* 40(4): 16–26.

Lazzarato, M. (2014). *Signs and Machines*. Los Angeles, CA., Semiotext(e).

Lindell, M. K. (2013). 'Disaster studies.' *Current Sociology* 61(5–6): 797–825.

Lindsay, J. R. (2003). 'The Determinants of Disaster Vulnerability Natural Hazards: Achieving Sustainable Mitigation through Population Health.' *Natural Hazards* 28(2–3): 291–304.

Linnebaugh, P. (2008). *The Magna Carta Manifesto*. Berkeley, CA., University of California Press.

Litman, T. (2006). 'Lessons from Katrina and Rita: What Major Disasters can teach Transportation Planners.' *Journal of Transportation Engineering* 132(1): 11–18.

Loewenstein, A. (2017). *Disaster Capitalism: Making a Killing Out of Catastrophe*. London; New York, Verso Books.

Lowe, D., K. L. Ebi and B. Forsberg. (2013). 'Factors Increasing Vulnerability to Health Effects before, during and after Floods.' *Int. J. Environ. Res. Public Health* 10(12), 7015–67.

Luxemburg, R. (2008). *The Essential Rosa Luxemburg. Reform or Revolution & The Mass Strike*. Chicago, Haymarket Books.

Marx, K. (1964) [1869]. *The Eighteenth Brumaire of Louis Bonaparte*. New York, International Publishers.

Marx, K. (1976) [1886]. *Capital Vol. I. A Critique of Political Economy*. Harmondsworth, Penguin.

Marx, K. (1984) [1932]. *The Economic & Philosophic Manuscripts of 1844*. Moscow, International Publishers.

Marx, K., F. Engels, C. J. Arthur and K. Marx (1970) [1932]. *The German Ideology. Part one*. New York, International Publishers.

Marx, K. and F. Engels (1975). *Karl Marx, Frederick Engels: Collected Works*. London, Lawrence & Wishart.

Maslin, S. (2013). 'Storm Effort Causes a Rift in a Shifting Occupy Movement.' *New York Times*. www.nytimes.com/2013/05/01/nyregion/occupy-movements-changing-focus-causes-rift.html (last accessed December 2019).

McNally, D. (2009). 'From Financial Crisis to World-Slump: Accumulation, Financialisation, and the Global Slowdown.' *Historical Materialism* 17(2): 35–83.

McNally, D. (2011). *Global Slump: The Economics and Politics of Crisis and Resistance*. Oakland, CA., PM Press.

Michney, T. M. (2007). 'Constrained Communities: Black Cleveland's Experience with World War II Public Housing.' *Journal of Social History* 40(4): 933–56.

Mileti, D. S. (1999). *Disasters by Design : A Reassessment of Natural Hazards in the United States*. Washington, D.C., Joseph Henry Press.

Mohandesi, S. and E. Teitelman (2017). 'Without Reserves.' in *Social Reproduction Theory: Remapping Class, Recentering Oppression*. T. Bhattacharya. London, Pluto Press: 37–67.

Moody, K. (2017). *How Capital is Reshaping the Battleground of Class War*. Chicago, IL., Haymarket.

Moss, D. (1999). 'Courting Disaster? The Transformation of Federal Disaster Policy since 1803.' in *The Financing of Catastrophe Risk*. K. Froot. Chicago, IL., University of Chicago Press: 307-362.

Murch, D. J. (2010). *Living for the City: Migration, Education, and the Rise of the Black Panther Party in Oakland, California*. Chapel Hill, University of North Carolina Press.

Neal, D. and B. D. Phillips (1995). 'Effective emergency management: Reconsidering the bureaucratic approach.' *Disasters* 19(4): 327–37.

Neocleous, M. (2013). 'Resisting resilience.' *Radical Philosophy* 178: 2–7.

Newton, H. P., D. Hilliard and D. Weise (2002). *The Huey P. Newton Reader*. New York, Seven Stories Press.

Nuzzo, J. B., L. Mullen, M. Snyder et al. (2019). 'Preparedness for a High-Impact Respiratory Pathogen Pandemic.' Johns Hopkins Center for Health Security. www.centerforhealthsecurity.org/our-work/pubs_archive/pubs-pdfs/2019/190918-GMPBreport-respiratorypathogen.pdf (last accessed July 2020).

O'Connor, J. R. (1998). *Natural Causes: Essays in Ecological Marxism*. New York, Guilford Press.

OECD, (2013). *Pensions at a Glance 2013: OECD and G20 Indicators*, OECD Publishing.

Office of Management and Budget (2016). *Budget of the U.S. Government. Fiscal Year 2017*, Washington, D.C., U.S. Government Printing Office.

Oran, S. S. (2017). 'Pensions and Social Reproduction.' in *Social Reproduction Theory: Remapping Class, Recentering Oppression*. T. Bhattacharya. London, Pluto Press: 148–71.

Out of the Wood's blog. (8 May 2014). 'Disaster communism part 1 – disaster communities.' *libcom.org*. http://libcom.org/blog/disaster-communism-part-1-disaster-communities-08052014. (last accessed December 2019).

Patel, S. S., M. B. Rogers, R. Amlôt et al. (2017). 'What Do We Mean by "Community Resilience?" A Systematic Literature Review of How It Is Defined in the Literature.' *PLOS Currents, Disasters*, 1 Feb 2017.

Patterson, O., F. Weil and K. Patel (2010). 'The Role of Community in Disaster Response: Conceptual Models.' *Population Research and Policy Review* 29: 127–41.

Perry, R. W. (2007). *What Is a Disaster? Handbook of Disaster Research*. H. Rodríguez, E. L. Quarantelli and R. R. Dynes. New York, Springer 1–15.

Pew Research Center. (2011). 'Wealth Gaps Rise to Record Highs between Whites, Blacks, Hispanics.' *Pew Research Center*. www.pewsocialtrends.org/2011/07/26/wealth-gaps-rise-to-record-highs-between-whites-blacks-hispanics/ (last accessed December 2019).

Pham, S. (2020). 'Police Arrested More Than 11,000 People At Protests Across The US.' *BuzzFeed News*. www.buzzfeednews.com/article/scottpham/floyd-protests-number-of-police-arrests (last accessed July 2020).

Pinkney, A. and R. R. Woock, (1970). *Poverty and Politics in Harlem*. New Haven, CT., New College & University Press.

Pinto, N. (2012). 'Hurricane Sandy is New York's Katrina.' *Village Voice*. www.villagevoice.com/news/hurricane-sandy-is-new-yorks-katrina-6436817. (last accessed December 2019).

Plyer, A. (2016). 'Facts for Features: Katrina Impact.' *The Data Center*. www.datacenterresearch.org/data-resources/katrina/facts-for-impact/ (last accessed December 2016).

Prince, S. H. (1920). *Catastrophe and Social Change, Based upon a Sociological Study of the Halifax Disaster*. New York, Columbia University Press.

Przeworski, A. (1985). *Capitalism and Social Democracy*. Cambridge, Cambridge University Press.

Quarantelli, E. L. (1978). *Disasters. Theory and Research*. Thousand Oaks, CA., Sage.

Radford Ruether, R. (2006). 'After Katrina: Poverty, Race and Environmental Degradation.' *Dialog* 45(2): 176–83.

Rand, M. R., J. P. Lynch and D. Cantor. (1997). 'National Crime Victimization Survey. Criminal Victimization, 1973–1995.' *Bureau of Justice Statistics*. https://pdfs.semanticscholar.org/77bd/0d613de2b1d38681466128d5b1ee1280c423.pdf (last accessed December 2019).

Rasmussen, M. B. (2015). *Crisis to Insurrection: Notes on the Ongoing Collapse*. Wivenhoe; New York; Port Watson, Autonomedia.

Rattner, N. and T. Higgins (2020). 'As new data shows early signs of economic recovery, black workers are being left out.' *CNBC*. www.cnbc.com/2020/06/05/coronavirus-recovery-black-workers-are-being-left-out-data-shows.html (last accessed July 2020).

Redford, P. (1970). *Billion-Dollar Sandbar; A Biography of Miami Beach*. New York, Dutton.

Reid, J. (2013). 'Interrogating the Neoliberal Biopolitics of the Sustainable Development-Resilience Nexus.' *International Political Sociology* 7(4): 353–67.

Revels, T. J. (2011). *Sunshine Paradise: A History of Florida Tourism*. Gainesville, FL., University Press of Florida.

Robbins, C. (2012). 'Occupy Sandy Recognized By NY Times, Mayor's Office & National Guard.' *Gothamist*. http://gothamist.com/2012/11/11/occupy_sandy_recognized_by_ny_times.php. (last accessed December 2019).

Rockefeller Foundation (2013). '100 Resilient Cities.' *The Rockefeller Foundation*. www.100resilientcities.org/#/-_/ (last accessed July 2019).

Rodin, J. (2014). *The Resilience Dividend: Being Strong in a World Where Things Go Wrong*. New York, Public Affairs.

Russill, C. and C. Lavin (2011). 'From Tipping Point to Meta-Crisis: Management, Media, and Hurricane Katrina.' in *The Neoliberal Deluge: Hurricane Katrina, Late Capitalism, and the Remaking of New Orleans*. C. Johnson. Minneapolis, MI., University of Minnesota Press: 3–31.

Schlanger, Z. (2020). 'Begging for Thermometers, Body Bags, and Gowns: U.S. Health Care Workers Are Dangerously Ill-Equipped to Fight Covid-19.' *Time*. https://time.com/5823983/coronavirus-ppe-shortage/ (last accessed July 2020).

Schmeltz, M., S. González, L. Fuentes, A. Kwan, A. Ortega-Williams and L. Cowan (2013). 'Lessons from Hurricane Sandy: a Community Response in Brooklyn, New York.' *Journal of Urban Health* 90(5): 799–809.

Schulman, L. (1982). 'The Decline and Fall of U.S. Steel: A Case Study in De-industrialization.' *Executive Intelligence Review* 9(32): 33–5.

Schwirtz, M. (2020). 'Nurses Die, Doctors Fall Sick and Panic Rises on Virus Front Lines.' *New York Times*. www.nytimes.com/2020/03/30/nyregion/ny-coronavirus-doctors-sick.html (last accessed July 2020).

Semenza, J. C., C. H. Rubin, K. H. Falter, J. D. Selanikio, W. D. Flanders, H. L. Howe and J. L. Wilhelm. (1996). 'Heat-Related Deaths during the July 1995 Heat Wave in Chicago.' *New England Journal of Medicine* 335(2): 84–90.

Shapiro, F. C. and J.W. Sullivan. (1964). *Race Riots, New York, 1964*. New York, Cromwell Company.

Solnit, R. (2009). *A Paradise Built in Hell*. Harmondsworth, Penguin.

Spangrud, T. (1987). *The United States Strategic Bombing Surveys European War Pacific War*. Maxwell, AL., DIANE Publishing.

Spencer, R. (2016). *The Revolution Has Come. Black Power, Gender, and the Black Panther Party in Oakland*. London; Durham, NC., Duke University Press.

Stallings, R. A. (1998). 'Disasters and the Theory of Social Order.' in *What is a Disaster? Perspectives on the Question*. E. L. Quarantelli. London; New York, Routledge: 127–46.

Stanley-Becker, I. (2018). 'Trump administration diverted nearly $10 million from FEMA to ICE detention program, according to DHS document.' *Washington Post*. www.washingtonpost.com/news/morning-mix/wp/2018/09/12/document-shows-the-trump-administration-diverted-nearly-10-million-from-fema-to-ice-detention-program/?noredirect=on&utm_term=.b6cbd7e11908. (last accessed January 2019).

Steinberg, T. (2000). *Acts of God: The Unnatural History of Natural Disaster in America*. New York, Oxford University Press.

Steinberg, T. (2014). *Gotham Unbound: The Ecological History of Greater New York*. New York, Simon & Schuster.

Stronge, W. B. (2008). *The Sunshine Economy: An Economic History of Florida Since the Civil War*. Gainesville, FL., University Press of Florida.

Sugrue, T. J. (1996). *The Origins of the Urban Crisis. Race and Inequality in Postwar Detroit*. Princeton, NJ., Princeton University Press.

Susman, P., P. O'Keefe and B. Wisner (1983). 'Global Disasters, A Radical Interpretation.' in *Interpretations of Calamity*. K. Hewitt. Boston, Mass., Allen and Unwin, 263–83.

Thompson, E. E. and N. Krause. (1998). 'Living Alone and Neighborhood Characteristics as Predictors of Social Support in Late Life.' *The Journals of Gerontology Series B: Psychological Sciences and Social Sciences* 53B(6): 354–64.

Tierney, K. (2006). 'Foreshadowing Katrina: Recent Sociological Contributions to Vulnerability Science.' *Contemporary Sociology* 35(3): 207–12.

Tierney, K. (2014). *The Social Roots of Risk: Producing Disasters, Promoting Resilience*. Stanford, CA., Stanford University Press.

Tierney, K. (2015). 'Resilience and the Neoliberal Project.' *American Behavioural Scientist* 59(10): 1327–42.

Tierney, K., C. Bevc and E. Kuligowski (2006). 'Metaphors matter: disaster myths, media frames, and their consequences in Hurricane Katrina.' *The Annals of the American Academy of Political and Social Science* 604(1): 57–81.

Tolentino, J. (2020). 'What Mutual Aid Can Do During a Pandemic.' *New Yorker*. www.newyorker.com/magazine/2020/05/18/what-mutual-aid-can-do-during-a-pandemic (last accessed July 2020).

Toscano, A. (2006). 'Dual Power Revisited: From Civil War to Biopolitical Islam.' *Soft Targets* 2(1): 150–55.

Toscano, A. (2009). 'Partisan Thought.' *Historical Materialism* 17(3): 175–91.

Toscano, A. (2014). 'Transition Deprogrammed.' *South Atlantic Quarterly* 113(4): 761.

Toscano, A. (2016). 'After October, Before February: Figures of Dual Power.' in *An American Utopia: Dual Power and the Universal Army*. F. Jameson and S. Žižek. London; New York, Verso.

Tronti, M. (2019). *Workers and Capital*. London; New York, Verso.

Trump, D. J. (2018). 'Budget of the U.S. Government. A New Foundation for American Greatness. Fiscal Year 2018.' *The White House*. www.whitehouse.gov/wp-content/uploads/2017/11/budget.pdf, (last accessed July 2019).

Twigg, J. and I. Mosel. (2017). 'Emergent groups and spontaneous volunteers in urban disaster response.' *Environment and Urbanization* 29(2): 443–58.

Vogel, L. (2013). *Marxism and the Oppression of Women: Toward a Unitary Theory*. Leiden, Brill.

Von Foerster, H. (2003). *Understanding Understanding: Essays on Cybernetics and Cognition*. New York, Springer.

Walker, A. (2008). 'Towards a Political Economy of Old Age.' *Ageing and Society* 1(1): 73–94.

Wark, M. (2015). *Molecular Red: Theory for the Anthropocene*. London; New York, Verso.

Warren, K. and J. Hadden (2020). 'How all 50 states are responding to the George Floyd protests, from imposing curfews to calling in the National Guard.' *Business Insider*. www.businessinsider.com/us-states-response-george-floyd-protests-curfews-national-guard-2020-6?r=DE&IR=T (last accessed July 2020).

Warzel, C. (2020). 'Feeling Powerless About Coronavirus? Join a Mutual-Aid Network.' *New York Times*. www.nytimes.com/2020/03/23/opinion/coronavirus-aid-group.html (last accessed July 2020).

Weaver, C. (2012). 'Post-Storm, "Occupy Wall Street" becomes "Occupy Sandy."' *Voice of America*. www.voanews.com/usa/post-storm-occupy-wall-street-becomes-occupy-sandy (last accessed December 2019).

Weizman, E. (2011). *The Least of All Possible Evils: Humanitarian Violence from Arendt to Gaza*. London; New York, Verso.

Williams, E. C. (2011). 'Fire to the Commons.' in *Communization and its Discontents: Contestation, Critique and Contemporary Struggles*. B. Noys. Wivenhoe, New York, Port Watson, Minor Compositions: 175–95.

Williams, H. B. (1954). 'Fewer Disasters, Better Studied.' *Journal of Social Issues* 10(3): 5–11.

Wilson Gilmore, R. (2002). 'Race and Globalization.' in *Geographies of Global Change: Remapping the World*, R. J. Johnston, Peter J. Taylor, and Michael J. Watts, Malden, Mass., Blackwell.

Wilson Gilmore, R. (2007). *Golden Gulag. Prisons, Surplus, Crisis, and Opposition in Globalizing California*. Berkeley, CA., University of California Press.

Wilson, V. (2016). 'Black workers' wages have been harmed by both widening racial wage gaps and the widening productivity-pay gap.' *Economic Policy Institute*. www.epi.org/files/pdf/115812.pdf (last accessed December 2019).

Wisner, B. (2004). 'Assessment of Capability and Vulnerability.' in *Mapping Vulnerability: Disasters, Development, and People*. G. Bankoff, G. Frerks and D. Hilhorst. London; Sterling, VA, Earthscan Publications: 183–93.

Wisner, B., J. C. Gaillard and I. Kelman (2012). *The Routledge Handbook of Hazards and Distaster Risk Reduction*. New York, Routledge.

Woodcock, J. (2014), 'The Worker's Inquiry from Trotskyism to Operaismo: A Political Methodology for Investigating the Workplace.' *Ephemera. Theory & Politics in Organization* 14(3), 493–513.

Wright Mills, C. (1960). 'Letter to the New Left.' *New Left Review* 5. www.marxists.org/subject/humanism/mills-c-wright/letter-new-left.htm (last accessed December 2019).

Wu, J., A. McCann, J. Katz et al. (2020). '153,000 Missing Deaths: Tracking the True Toll of the Coronavirus Outbreak.' *New York Times*. www.nytimes.com/interactive/2020/04/21/world/coronavirus-missing-deaths.html (last accessed July 2020).

Index

Thanks to our Patreon Subscribers:

Abdul Alkalimat
Andrew Perry

Who have shown their generosity and
comradeship in difficult times.